The World's Worst Poet

Selections from "Poetic Gems"
by William McGonagall with an appreciation by
James O. Jackson, *The Chicago Tribune*

An Octavo Press Book
distributed by
Templegate Publishers

ISBN: 87243-088-X

Published by
Templegate Publishers
302 East Adams Street
Springfield, Illinois 62701

Table of Contents

An Appreciation

by James O. Jackson
Foreign Correspondent, The Chicago Tribune

Dundee, Scotland — One summer nearly one hundred years ago an impoverished weaver, sitting alone in a shabby Dundee room, felt overcome by what he called "a strong desire to write poetry."

The weaver, named William McGonagall was by no means the first man ever to be visited by the muse. Nor was he the last. But the poetry inspired by that summertime urge made McGonagall immortal: it is the worst ever written, in any language, at any time.

He stands unique and unchallenged as history's worst poet, and during the centenary year of his inspiration there was a worldwide revival of interest in the man and his work.

Scholars in Thailand have translated the best of his bad ditties; professors in Kiev, Hong Kong, Bucharest, London, and Lansing, Michigan, have ordered copies of his works for use in their literature courses; dinners have been staged in his memory; a monument is being commissioned, and his doggerel has been recited and read in smoky pubs from Glasgow to Sydney.

"The man was unique, there's no doubt about that," said William Smith, a Dundee printer who is the leading expert on McGonagall and his works. "There's a perfection, after all, in being the worst there is. Nobody has ever been able to match his bad verse. People have tried, but they can't do it."

Smith said that McGonagall was at the best of his worst, or the worst of his best, when memorializing fires, shipwrecks, and suicides. He seemed to be inspired by disasters, and one of his finest bad poems was a 10-stanza account of a blaze in Glasgow that began:

'Twas in the year of 1888, and on October the
    fourteenth day,
That a fire broke out in a warehouse, and for hours
    blazed away;
And the warehouse, now destroyed, was occupied by the
    Messrs. R. Wylie, Hill and Co.,
Situated in Buchanan Street, in the city of Glasgow.

McGonagall's acknowledged masterwork was his account of the Tay Bridge disaster in 1879. The great railway bridge across the Tay was regarded as something of an engineering marvel when it was built some years earlier, and McGonagall had commemorated its completion with a verse that includes the lines:

I hope that God will protect all passengers by night
    and by day,
And that no accident befall them while crossing the bridge
    of the silvery Tay,
For that would be most awful to be seen
Near by Dundee and the Magdalen green.

McGonagall recited the rhyme in a pub, and despite some catcalling and guffaws he remarked later that he thought the poem "went down well."

Unfortunately, so did the bridge. It collapsed during a storm while a passenger train was crossing over, dumping the train into the stormy waters with heavy loss of life. McGonagall was up to the event. Soon he was rising in public houses to intone:

Beautiful railway bridge of the silv'ry Tay!
Alas I am very sorry to say
That 90 lives have been taken away on the last Sabbath
    day of 1879,
Which will be remember'd for a very long time.

It was of such bumbling meter and crippled rhyme that McGonagall's immortality was made. Nobody has been able to duplicate it.

In 1965, two British oil companies organized a competition to find out whether anyone could write poetry as badly as he did, with cash prizes for those who could measure up, or down, to the great McGonagall. There were dozens of entries, but a panel of judges (which included Peter Sellers and Spike Milligan) declared no winner. None, they said, were bad enough.

But for all the laughter and foolery surrounding McGonagall, there is more to his immortality than bad poetry. There is an attraction about the man himself: he was a genuine eccentric, a man of such honesty and sincerity of purpose, that his readers cannot help but admire him. Those who open a book of his verse find themselves reading on and on. They like it. They like him.

"He believed in his heart he was a great poet," said the printer Smith. "He believed that he should succeed Lord Tennyson as the Poet Laureate, and he was so serious about it that he walked all the way to Balmoral Castle to ask Queen Victoria to choose him. He wasn't even allowed inside the gates, of course, and he had to walk all the way back."

But McGonagall bore his queen no ill will. He wrote a number of verses to her, rising to particularly remarkable heights of stumbling scansion when a man named Maclean tried to assassinate her.

God prosper long our noble queen, and long may
    she reign!
Maclean he tries to shoot her, but it was all in vain.
For God he turned the ball aside Maclean aimed at
    her head;
And he felt very angry because he didn't shoot her dead.

Not surprisingly, McGonagall suffered greatly for his pains. He could not make a living from his poems, and he was constantly in debt, being sued several times for unpaid grocery bills and eventually dying a pauper in Glasgow.

But most painful were the hoaxes and jokes played on him. When he attempted to recite in pubs, the rowdy drinkers often threw food or shouted coarse jokes. On one occasion he was pelted with peas when he tried to sing one of his songs, and on another, one of his recitals ended abruptly when the revelers dumped a sack of flour over him.

He was frequently the target of hoax letters, and his

simplicity was such that he often accepted them as genuine. A group of Edinburgh students once concocted a letter from the "King of Burma" which praised McGonagall's poetry and declared him a "Knight of the Order of the White Elephant of Burma." The honorific included a gift of a topaz, the "gem of lowest value," intended as a joke, mocking the title of McGonagall's first book of verse, "Poetic Gems."

But to him, the letter seemed not at all bizarre. From then on, he signed himself as "Sir William Topaz McGonagall," and he sincerely believed himself to be a Burmese knight.

For all his sufferings, McGonagall had a number of genuine friends who helped keep his wife and children from starving and who helped him publish his poems. The Rev. George Gilfillan, a prominent Dundee clergyman, took a kindly interest in the eccentric weaver's troubles, and in gratitude McGonagall wrote one of his earliest verses about the preacher.

Rev. George Gilfillan of Dundee, there is none can
    you excel;
You have boldly rejected the confession of faith, and
    defended your cause right well.
The first time I heard him speak, 'twas in the
    Kinnaird Hall,
Lecturing on the Garibaldi movement, as loud as he
    could bawl.

The Rev. Mr. Gilfillan, on reading the tribute from his friend, remarked with gentle truth:
    "Shakespeare never wrote anything like this."
    "It's easy for us to laugh at him," Smith said. "But

keep in mind that this was an extremely poor man, with only 18 months of formal education. He lived at a time when men of his class simply did not receive letters, and if they did, they could not read them. He was able to read and write, and that was a tremendous accomplishment. I think he was a genius."

Smith said McGonagall's verse today has a special appeal to Asians and East Europeans, many of whom seem to accept his poetry as work of consequence.

"I think he appeals to the Eastern mind because he's simple and straightforward," Smith said. "Anyway, how does one judge genius? Look at Picasso — if you brought me a Picasso 40 years ago, I'd have thrown it in the trash."

And, too, how does one judge greatness?

Smith said McGonagall has achieved a fame and exposure that very few poets achieve. Professors of English in universities throughout Eastern Europe, including the Universities of Moscow, Warsaw, and Kiev, have ordered thousands of copies of McGonagall's poems. Japanese, Thai, Singaporese, and Chinese scholars have translated McGonagall into their languages, and his poems have been rendered in Russian, Bulgarian, and Romanian.

Earlier in 1977 a centenary dinner was held in his memory in Dundee, and McGonagall devotees are planning to erect a commemorative monument in the Dundee park he frequented.

Smith said that 500,000 copies of "Poetic Gems" have been sold, and the volume is reprinted every year. It is a rare poet whose works have been so widely published so long after his death.

"McGonagall's fondest dream was to succeed Lord Tennyson as Poet Laureate, and of course that never happened," Smith said.

Who did succeed Lord Tennyson? Alfred Austin. Who ever heard of Alfred Austin?

Brief Autobiography

Dear Reader, —My parents were both born in Ireland, where they spent the great part of their lives after their marriage. They left Ireland for Scotland, and never returned to the Green Isle. I was born in the year of 1830 in the city of Edinburgh, the garden of bonnie Scotland, which is justly famed by all for its magnificent scenery. My parents were poor, but honest, sober, and God-fearing. My father was a hand-loom weaver, and wrought at cotton fabrics during his stay in Edinburgh, which was for about two years. Owing to the great depression in the cotton trade in Edinburgh, he removed to Paisley with his family, where work was abundant for a period of about three years; but then a crash taking place, he was forced to remove to Glasgow with his family with the hope of securing work there, and enable him to support his young and increasing family, as they were all young at that time, your humble servant included. In Glasgow he was fortunate in getting work as a cotton weaver; and as trade was in a prosperous state for about two years, I was sent to school, where I remained about eighteen months, but at the expiry of which, trade again becoming dull, my poor parents were compelled to take me from school, being unable to pay for schooling through adverse circumstances; so that all the education I received was before I was seven years of age.

My father, being forced to leave Glasgow through want of work, came to Dundee, where plenty of work was to be had at the time — such as sacking, cloth, and other fabrics. It was at this time that your humble servant was sent to work in a mill in the Scouringburn, which was owned by Mr Peter Davie, and there I remained for about four years, after which I was taken from the mill, and put to learn the handloom in Ex-Provost Reid's factory, which was also situated in the Scouringburn. After I had learned to be an expert hand-loom weaver, I began to take a great delight in reading books, as well as to improve my hand-writing, in my leisure hours at night, until I made myself what I am.

The books that I liked best to read were Shakespeare's penny plays, more especially Macbeth, Richard III, Hamlet, and Othello; and I gave myself no rest until I obtained complete mastery over the above four characters. Many a time in my dear father's absence I enacted entire scenes from Macbeth and Richard III, along with some of my shopmates, until they were quite delighted; and many a time they regaled me and the other actors that had entertained them to strong ale, biscuits, and cheese.

My first appearance on any stage was in Mr Giles' theatre, which was in Lindsay Street quarry, some years ago; I cannot give the exact date, but it is a very long time ago. The theatre was built of brick, somewhat similar to Mr M'Givern's at the top of Seagate. The character that I appeared in was Macbeth, Mrs Giles sustaining the character of Lady Macbeth on that occasion, which she performed admirably. The way that I was allowed to perform was in terms of the following agreement, which was entered into between Mr Giles and myself—that I had to give Mr Giles one pound in cash before the performance, which I considered rather hard, but as there was no help for it, I made known Mr Giles's terms to my shopmates, who were handloom weavers in Seafield Works, Taylor's Lane. No sooner than the terms were made known to them, than they entered heartily into the arrangement, and in a very short time they made up the pound by subscription, and with one accord declared they would go and see me perform the Thane of Fife, *alias* Macbeth. To see that the arrangement with Mr Giles was carried out to the letter, a deputation of two of my shopmates was appointed to wait upon him with the pound. Mr Giles received the deputation, and on receipt of the money cheerfully gave a written agreement certifying that he would allow me to perform Macbeth on the following night in his theatre. When the deputation came back with the news that Mr Giles had consented to allow me to make my *debut* on the following night, my shopmates cheered again and again, and the rapping of the lays I will never forget as long as I live. When the great night arrived my shopmates were in high glee with the hope of getting a Shakespearian treat from your humble servant. And I can assure you, without boasting, they were not disappointed in their anticipations, my shopmates having secured seats before the general public were admitted. It would be impossible for me to describe the scene in Lindsay Street, as it was crowded from head to foot, all being eager to witness my first appearance as an exponent of Shakespeare. When I appeared on the stage I was received with a perfect storm of applause, but when I exclaimed "Command, they make a halt upon the heath," the applause was deafening, and was continued during the entire evening, especially so in the combat scene. The house was crowded during each of the three performances on that ever-memorable night, which can never be forgot by me or my shopmates, and even entire strangers included. At the end of each performance I was called before the curtain, and received plaudit after plaudit of applause in recognition of my able impersonation of Macbeth.

What a sight it was to see such a mass of people struggling to gain admission! Hundreds failing to do so, and in the struggle numbers were trampled under foot, one man having lost one of his shoes in the scrimmage; others were carried bodily into the theatre along with the press. So much then for the true account of my first appearance on any stage.

The most startling incident in my life was the time I discovered myself to be a poet, which was in the year 1877. During the Dundee holiday week, in the bright and balmy month of June, when trees and flowers were in full bloom, while lonely and sad in my room, I sat thinking about the thousands of people who were away by rail and steamboat, perhaps to the land of Burns, or poor ill-treated Tannahill, or to gaze upon the Trossachs in Rob Roy's country, or elsewhere wherever their minds led them. Well, while pondering so, I seemed to feel as it were a strange kind of feeling stealing over me, and remained so for about five minutes. A flame, as Lord Byron has said, seemed to kindle up my entire frame, along with a strong desire to write poetry; and I felt so happy, so happy, that I was inclined to dance, then I began to pace backwards and forwards in the room, trying to shake off all thought of writing poetry; but the more I tried, the more strong the sensation became. It was so strong, I imagined that a pen was in my right hand, and a voice crying,

"Write!" "Write!" So I said to myself, ruminating, let me see; what shall I write? Then all at once a bright idea struck me to write about my best friend, the late Reverend George Gilfillan; in my opinion I could not have chosen a better subject, therefore I immediately found paper, pen, and ink, and set myself down to immortalize the great preacher, poet, and orator. These are the lines I penned, which I dropped into the box of the *Weekly News* office surreptitiously, which appeared in that paper as follows:—

"W. M'G., Dundee, who modestly seeks to hide his light under a bushel, has surreptitiously dropped into our letterbox an address to the Rev. George Gilfillan. Here is a sample of this worthy's powers of versification: —

'Rev. George Gilfillan of Dundee,
    There is none can you excel;
You have boldly rejected the Confession of Faith,
    And defended your cause right well.

'The first time I heard him speak,
    'Twas in the Kinnaird Hall,
Lecturing on the Garibaldi movement,
    As loud as he could bawl.

'He is a liberal gentleman
    To the poor while in distress,
And for his kindness unto them
    The Lord will surely bless.

'My blessing on his noble form,
    And on his lofty head,

16

May all good angels guard him while living,
    And hereafter when he's dead.' "*

P.S.—This is the first poem that I composed while under the divine inspiration, and is true, as I have to give an account to God at the day of judgment for all the sins I have committed.

With regard to my far-famed Balmoral journey, I will relate it truly as it happened. 'Twas on a bright summer morning in the month of July 1878, I left Dundee *en route* for Balmoral, the Highland home of Her Most Gracious Majesty, Queen of Great Britain and Empress of India. Well, my first stage for the day was the village of Alyth. When I arrived there I felt weary, foot-sore, and longed for rest and lodgings for the night. I made enquiry for a good lodging-house, and found one very easily, and for the lodging I paid fourpence to the landlady before I sat down, and when I had rested my weary limbs for about five minutes I rose and went out to purchase some provisions for

---

* EDITOR'S NOTE: Gilfillan's estimate of McGonagall was somewhat more restrained. "I certify," said the Rev. Gilfillan in response to McGonagall's request for a testimonial, "that William McGonagall has for some time been known to me. I have heard him speak, he has a strong proclivity for the elocutionary department, a strong voice, and great enthusiasm. He has had a good deal of experience, too, having addressed audiences and enacted parts here and elsewhere."

A testimonial only slightly more enthusiastic was provided by a trio of Dundee elders:

We willingly certify that the bearer, Mr. William McGonagall, has considerable ability in recitation. We have heard him recite some passages from Shakespeare with great force; and are of opinion that he is quite competent to read or recite passages from the poets and orators in villages and country towns with pleasure and profit to his audience. We also believe him to be a respectable man.

Islay Burns, Minister of St. Peter's F. Church
John Alex. Banks, M.A., Edin., Headmaster, Propy. School, Dundee
William Knight, Assistant, Free St. John's Ch., Dundee
(now professor, St. Andrew's University)

29th March, 1864

my supper and breakfast—some bread, tea, sugar, and butter—when I had purchased the provisions I returned to my lodgings and prepared for myself a hearty tea, which I relished very much, I can assure you, for I felt very hungry, not having tasted food of any kind by the way during my travel, which caused me to have a ravenous appetite, and to devour it greedily; and after supper I asked the landlady to oblige me with some water to wash my feet, which she immediately and most cheerfully supplied me with; then I washed my sore blistered feet and went to bed, and was soon in the arms of Morpheus, the god of sleep. Soundly I slept all the night, until the landlady awoke me in the morning, telling me it was a fine sunshiny morning. Well, of course I arose, and donned my clothes, and I felt quite refreshed after the refreshing sleep I had got during the night; then I gave myself a good washing, and afterwards prepared my breakfast, which I devoured quickly, and left the lodging-house, bidding the landlady good morning, and thanking her for her kindness then I wended my way the next day as far as the Spittal o' Glenshee—

Which is the most dismal to see—
With its bleak, rocky mountains,
And clear, crystal fountains,
With their misty foam;
And thousands of sheep there together do roam,
Browsing on the barren pasture, blasted-like to see,
Stunted in heather, and scarcely a tree;
And black-looking cairns of stones, as monuments
    to show,
Where people have been found that were lost in
    the snow—

Which is cheerless to behold—
And as the traveller gazes thereon it makes his blood
    run cold,
And almost makes him weep,
For a human voice is seldom heard there,
Save the shepherd crying to his sheep.

The chains of mountains there is most frightful to see,
Along each side of the Spittal o' Glenshee;
But the Castleton o' Braemar is most beautiful to see,
With its handsome whitewashed houses, and romantic
    scenery,
And bleak-looking mountains, capped with snow,
Where the deer and the roe do ramble to and fro,
Near by the dark river Dee,
Which is most beautiful to see.

And Balmoral Castle is magnificent to be seen,
Highland home of the Empress of India, Great Britain's
    Queen,
With its beautiful pine forests, near by the river Dee,
Where the rabbits and hares do sport in mirthful glee,
And the deer and the roe together do play
All the live long summer day,
In sweet harmony together,
While munching the blooming heather,
With their hearts full of glee,
In the green woods of Balmoral, near by the river Dee.

And, my dear friends, when I arrived at the Spittal o'
Glenshee, a dreadful thunder-storm came on, and the vi-
vid flashes of the forked lightning were fearful to behold,
and the rain poured down in torrents until I was drenched

to the skin, and longed to be under cover from the pitiless rain. Still God gave me courage to proceed on my weary journey, until I arrived at a shepherd's house near by the wayside, and I called at the house, as God had directed me to do, and knocked at the door fearlessly. I was answered by the servant maid, who asked me kindly what I wanted, and I told her I wanted lodgings for the night, and that I was wet to the skin with the rain, and that I felt cold and hungry, and that I would feel thankful for any kind of shelter for the night, as it was still raining and likely to be for the night. Then she told me there was no accommodation; then the shepherd himself came to the door, and he asked me what I wanted, and I told him I wanted a lodging for the night, and at first he seemed unwilling, eyeing me with a suspicious look, perhaps taking me for a burglar, or a sheep-stealer, who had come to steal his sheep — at least that was my impression. But when I showed him Her Most Gracious Majesty's royal letter, with the royal black seal, that I had received from her for my poetic abilities, he immediately took me by the hand and bade me come in, and told me to "gang in ower to the fire and to warm mysel'," at the same time bidding the servant maid make some supper ready for the poet; and while the servant girl was making some porridge for me, I showed him a copy of my poems, which I gave to him as a present for his kindness towards me, which he read during the time I was taking my supper, and seemed to appreciate very much. Then when I had taken my supper, he asked me if I would be afraid to sleep in the barn, and I told him so long as I put my trust in God I had nought to fear, and that these were the principles my dear parents had taught me. When I told him so he felt quite delighted, and bade me warm my feet before I would "gang oot to my bed i' the barn," and when I had warmed my feet, he accompanied me to the barn, where there was a bed that might have pleased Her Most Gracious Majesty, and rolling down the bed-clothes with his own hands, he wished me a sound sleep, and bade me good-night. Then I instantly undressed and tumbled into bed, and was soon sound asleep, dreaming that I saw Her Most Gracious Majesty riding in her carriage-and-pair, which was afterwards truly verified. Well, when I awoke the next morning I felt rather chilled, owing to the wetting I had got, and the fatigue of the distance I had travelled; but, nothing daunted, I still resolved to see Her Majesty. So I dressed myself quickly, and went over to the house to bid the shepherd good-morning, and thank him for the kindness I had received at his hands, but I was told by the girl he was away tending the sheep, but that he had told her to give me my breakfast, and she bade me come in and sit down and get it. So of course I went in, and got a good breakfast of porridge and good Highland milk, enough to make a hungry soul to sing with joy, especially in a strange country, and far from home. Well, having breakfasted, I arose and bade the servant girl good-bye, at the same time thanking her and the shepherd — her master — for their kindness towards me. Then, taking to the road again, I soon came in sight of the Castleton o' Braemar, with its beautiful whitewashed houses and romantic scenery, which I have referred to in my poem. When I arrived at the Castleton o' Braemar it was near twelve o'clock noon, and from the Castleton it is twelve miles to Balmoral; and I arrived at the lodge gates of the palace of Balmoral just as the tower clock chimed three; and when I crossed the little bridge that spans the river Dee, which has been erected by Her Majesty, I walked boldly forward and knocked loudly at the porter lodge door, and it was immediately answered by the two constables that are there night and day, and one of them asked me in a very authoritative tone what I wanted, and of course I told him I wanted to see Her Majesty, and he repeated, "Who do you want to see?" and I said I was surprised to think that he should ask me again after telling him distinctly that I wanted to see Her Majesty. Then I showed him Her Majesty's royal letter of patronage for my poetic abilities, and he read it, and said it was not Her Majesty's letter; and I said, "Whose is it then? do you take me for a forger?" Then he said Sir Thomas Biddulph's signature was not on the letter, but I told him it was on the envelope, and he looked and found it to be so. Then he said, "Why didn't you tell me that before?" I said I forgot. Then he asked me what I wished him to do with the letter, and I requested him to show it to Her Majesty or Sir Thomas Biddulph. He left me, pretending to go up to the palace with the letter, standing out in the cold in front of the lodge, wondering if he would go up to the palace as he pretended. However, be that as it may, I know not, but he returned with an answer as follows: — "Well, I've been up at the Castle with your letter, and the answer I got for you is they cannot be bothered with you," said with great vehemence. "Well," I replied, "It cannot be helped"; and he said it could not, and began to question me when I left Dundee, and the way I had come from Dundee, and where I had lodged by the way; and I told him, and he noted it all down in his memorandum book, and when he had done so he told me I would have to go back home again the same way I came; and then he asked me if I had brought any of my poetry with me, and I said I had, and showed him the second edition, of which I had several copies, and he looked at the front of it, which seemed to arrest his attention, and said, "You are not poet to Her Majesty; Tennyson's the real poet to Her Majesty." Then I said, "Granted; but, sir, you cannot deny that I have received Her Majesty's patronage." Then he said, "I should like very much to hear you give some specimens of your abilities," and I said, "Where?" and he said, "Just where you stand"; and I said, "No, sir, nothing so degrading in the open air. When I give specimens of my abilities it is either in a theatre or some hall, and if you want to hear me take me inside of the lodge, and pay me before I begin; then you shall hear me. These are my conditions, sir; do you accept my terms?" Then he said, "Oh, you might to oblige the young lady there." So I looked around to see the young lady he referred to, and there she was, looking out at the lodge entrance; and when I saw her I said, "No, sir, I will not; if it were Her Majesty's request I wouldn't do it in the open air, far less do it to please the young lady." Then the lady shut the lodge door, and he said, "Well, what do you charge for this book of poems?" and I said "2d.," and he gave it me, telling me to go straight home and not to think of coming back again to Balmoral. So I bade him good-bye and retraced my steps in search of a lodging for the night, which I obtained at the first farmhouse I called at; and when I knocked at the door I was told to come in and warm my feet at the fire, which I accordingly did, and when I told the good wife and man who I was, and about me being at the palace, they felt very much for me, and lodged me for the night, and fed me likewise, telling me to stay with them for a day or two, and go to the roadside and watch Her Majesty, and speak to her, and that I might be sure she would do something for me, but I paid no heed to their advice. And when I had got my supper, I was shown out to the barn by the gudeman, and there was prepared for me a bed which might have done a prince, and the gudeman bade me goodnight. So I closed the barn door and went to bed, resolving to be up very early the next morning and on the road, and with the thought thereof I couldn't sleep. So as soon as daylight appeared, I got up and donned my clothes, and went to the farmer's door and knocked, for they had not arisen, it being so early, and I bade them good-bye, thanking them at the same time for their kindness; and in a few minutes I was on the road again for Dundee — it being Thursday morning I refer to — and lodging in the same houses on my homeward journey, which I accomplished in three days, by arriving in Dundee on Saturday early in the day, foot-sore and weary, but not the least discouraged. So ends my ever-memorable journey to Balmoral.

My next adventure was going to New York, America, in the year 1887, March the 10th. I left Glasgow on board the beautiful steamer "Circassia," and had a very pleasant voyage for a fortnight at sea; and while at sea I was quite a favourite amongst the passengers, and displayed my histronic abilities, to the delight of the passengers, but received no remuneration for doing; but I was well pleased with the diet I received; also with the kind treatment I met with from the captain and chief steward — Mr Hendry. When I arrived at Castle Garden, New York, I wasn't permitted to pass on to my place of destination until the officials there questioned me regarding the place in New York I was going to, and how old I was, and what trade I was; and, of course, I told them I was a weaver, whereas if I had said I was a poet, they wouldn't allowed me to pass, but I satisfied them in their interrogations, and was allowed to pass on to my place of destination. During my stay in New York with a Dundee man, I tried occasionally to get an engagement from theatrical proprietors and music-hall proprietors, But alas! 'twas all in vain, for they all told me they didn't encourage rivalry, but if I had the money to secure a hall to display my abilities, or a company of my own, I would make lots of money; but I am sorry to say I had neither, therefore I considered wisely it was time to leave, so I wrote home to a Dundee gentleman requesting him to take me home, and he granted my request cheerfully, and secured for me a passage on board the "Circassia" again, and I had a very pleasant return voyage home again to bonnie Dundee. Since I came home to Dundee I have been very well treated by the more civilised community, and have made several appearances before the public in Baron Zeigler's circus and Transfield's circus, to delighted and crowded audiences; and the more that I was treated unkindly by a few ignorant boys and the Magistrates of the city, nevertheless my heart still clings to Dundee; and, while in Glasgow, my thoughts, night and day, were always towards Dundee; yet I must confess, during a month's stay in Glasgow, I gave three private entertainments to crowded audiences, and was treated like a prince by them, but owing to declining health, I had to leave the city of Glasgow. Since this Book of Poems perhaps will be my last effort,—

I earnestly hope the inhabitants of the beautiful city
   of Dundee
Will appreciate this little volume got up by me,
And when they read its pages, I hope it will fill their hearts
   with delight,
While seated around the fireside on a cold winter's night;
And some of them, no doubt, will let a silent tear fall
In dear remembrance of

WILLIAM McGONAGALL.

Reminiscenses

My Dearly Beloved Readers, —I will begin with giving an account of my experiences amongst the publicans. Well, I must say that the first man who threw peas at me was a publican, while I was giving an entertainment to a few of my admirers in a public-house in a certain little village not far from Dundee; but, my dear friends, I wish it to be understood that the publican who threw the peas at me was not the landlord of the public-house, he was one of the party who came to hear me give my entertainment. Well, my dear readers, it was while I was singing my own song, "The Rattling Boy from Dublin Town," that he threw the peas at me. You must understand that the Rattling Boy was courting a lass called Biddy Brown, and the Rattling Boy chanced to meet his Biddy one night in company with another lad called Barney Magee which, of course, he did not like to see, and he told Biddy he considered it too bad for her to be going about with another lad, and he would bid her good-bye for being untrue to him. Then Barney Magee told the Rattling Boy that Biddy Brown was his lass, and that he could easily find another — and come and have a glass, and be friends. But the Rattling Boy told Barney Magee to give his glass of strong drink to the devil! meaning, I suppose, it was only fit for devils to make use of, not for God's creatures. Because, my friends, too often has strong drink been the cause of seducing many a beautiful young woman away from her true lover, and from her parents also, by a false seducer, which, no doubt, the Rattling Boy considered Barney Magee to be. Therefore, my dear friends, the reason, I think, for the publican throwing the peas at me is because I say, to the devil with your glass, in my song, "The Rattling Boy from Dublin," and he, no doubt, considered it had a teetotal tendency about it, and, for that reason, he had felt angry, and had thrown the peas at me.

My dear readers, my next adventure was as follows: — During the Blue Ribbon Army movement in Dundee, and on the holiday week of the New-year, I was taken into a public-house by a party of my friends, after the party had got a little refreshment, and myself along with the rest, they proposed that I should give them a little entertainment, which I most willingly consented to do, knowing I would be remunerated by the company for so doing, which was the case; the money I received from them I remember amounted to four shillings and sixpence. All had gone on as smoothly as a marriage ball, and every one of the party seemed to be highly delighted with the entertainment I had given them. Of course, you all ought to know that while singing a good song, or giving a good recitation, it helps to arrest the company's attention from the drink; yes! in many cases it does, my friends. Such at least, was the case with me — at least the publican thought so — for — what do you think? — he devised a plan to bring my entertainment to an end abruptly, and the plan was, he told the waiter to throw a wet towel at me, which, of course, the waiter did, as he was told, and I received the wet towel, full force, in the face, which staggered me, no doubt, and had the desired effect of putting an end to me giving any more entertainments in his house. But, of course, the company I had been entertaining felt angry with the publican for being guilty of such a base action towards me, and I felt indignant myself, my friends, and accordingly I left the company I had been entertaining and bade them good-bye. My dear friends, a publican is a creature that would wish to decoy all the money out of the people's pockets that enter his house; he does not want them to give any of their money away for an intellectual entertainment. No, no! by no means; give it all to him, and crush out entertainment altogether, thereby he would make more money if he could only do so. My dear friends, if there were more theatres in society than public-houses, it would be a much better world to live in, at least more moral; and oh! my dear friends, be advised by me. Give your money to the baker, and the butcher, also the shoe-maker and the clothier, and shun the publicans; give them no money at all, for this sufficient reason, they would most willingly deprive us of all moral entertainment if we would be as silly as to allow them. They would wish us to think only about what sort of strong drink we should make use of, and to place our affections on that only, and give the most of our earnings to them; no matter whether your families starve or not, or go naked or shoeless; they care not, so as their own families are well clothed from the cold, and well fed. My dear friends, I most sincerely entreat of you to shun the publicans as you would shun the devil, because nothing good can emanate from indulging in strong drink, but only that which is evil. Turn ye, turn ye! why be a slave to the bottle? Turn to God, and He will save you.

I hope the day is near at hand,
When strong drink will be banished from our land.

I remember a certain publican in the city that always pretended to have a great regard for me. Well, as I chanced to be passing by his door one day he was standing in the doorway, and he called on me to come inside, and, as he had been in the habit of buying my poetry, he asked me if I was getting on well, and, of course, I told him the truth, that I was not getting on very well, that I had nothing to do, nor I had not been doing anything for three weeks past, and, worse than all, I had no poetry to sell. Then he said that was a very bad job, and that he was very sorry to hear it, and he asked me how much I would take to give an entertainment in his large back-room, and I told him the least I would take would be five shillings. Oh! very well, he replied, I will invite some of my friends and acquaintances for Friday night first, and mind, you will have to be here at seven o'clock punctual to time, so as not to keep the company waiting. So I told him I would remember the time, and thanked him for his kindness, and bade him good-bye. Well, when Friday came, I was there punctually at seven o'clock, and, when I arrived, he told me I was just in time, and that there was a goodly company gathered to hear me. So he bade me go ben to the big room, and that he would be ben himself — as I supposed more to look after the money than to hear me give my entertainment. Well, my readers, when I made my appearance before the company I was greeted with applause, and they told me they had met together for the evening to hear me give my entertainment. Then a round of drink was called for, and the publican answered the call. Some of the company had whisky to drink, and others had porter or ale, whichever they liked best; as for myself, I remember I had gingerbeer. Well, when we had all partaken of a little drink, it was proposed by some one in the company that a chairman should be elected for the evening, which seemed to meet with the publican's approbation. Then the chairman was elected, and I was introduced to the company by the chairman as the great poet McGonagall, who was going to give them an entertainment from his own productions; hoping they would keep good order and give me a fair hearing, and, if they would, he was sure I would please them. And when he had delivered himself so, he told me to begin, and accordingly I did so, and entertained the company for about an hour and a half. The company was highly satisfied with the entertainment I gave them, and everyone in the company gave threepence each, or sixpence each — whatever they liked, I suppose — until it amounted to five shillings. Then the chairman told the publican that five shillings had been subscribed anent the entertainment I had given, and handed it to him. Then the publican gave it to me, and I thanked him and the company for the money I received from them anent the entertainment I had given them. Then the chairman proposed that I should sing "The Rattling Boy from Dublin" over again, and that would conclude the evening's entertainment and that I would get another subscription, which was unanimously carried by the company, but opposed by the publican; and he told me and the company I had no right to get any more than I had bargained for. But, my friends, his motive for objecting to me getting any more money was to get it himself anent another round of drink he guessed the party would have after I left. And such was the case, as I was told by one of the party the next day, who stayed well up to eleven o'clock, and it was after ten o'clock when I left. Now, my friends, here was a man, a publican, I may say, that pretended to be my friend, that was not satisfied with the money that he got from the company for so many rounds of drink, all through me, of course, that had brought them there to hear me give an entertainment. My opinion is, if I had been as simple to have spent my five shillings that I got for giving my entertainment, he would not have felt satisfied either. In my opinion, he would have laughed at my simplicity for doing so. May heaven protect me from all such friends for ever, and protect everyone that reads my experiences amongst the publications in this little Book of Poetic Gems!

I remember another night while giving an entertainment in a certain public-house to my admirers, and as soon as the publican found out I was getting money for giving the entertainment, he immediately wrote a letter and addressed it to me, or caused some one else to do it for him, and one of the waiters gave it to me. As soon as I received it in my hand I gave it to one of the company to read, and before he broke open the letter I told him it was a hoax, in my opinion, got up to make me leave his house; and, my dear friends, it was just as I thought — a hoax. I was told in that letter, by particular request, to go to Gray's Hall, where a ball was held that evening, and, at the request of the master of the ceremonies, I was requested to come along to the hall, and recite my famous poem, "Bruce of Bannockburn" and I would be remunerated for it, and to hire a cab immediately, for the company at the ball were all very anxious to hear me. So I left the public-house directly, but I was not so foolish as to hire a cab to take me to Gray's Hall. No, my friends, I walked all the way, and called at the hall and shewed the letter to a man that was watching the hall door, and requested him to read it, and to show it to the master of the ball ceremonies, to see if I was wanted to recite my poem, "Bruce of Bannockburn." So the man took the letter from me and shewed it to the master of the ceremonies, and he soon returned with the letter, telling me it was a hoax, which I expected. My dear friends, this lets you see so far, as well as me, that these publicans that won't permit singing or reciting in their houses are the ones that are selfish or cunning. They know right well that while anyone is singing a song in the company, or reciting, it arrests the attention of the audience from off the drink. That is the reason, my dear friends, for the publican not allowing moral entertainments to be carried on in their houses, which I wish to impress on your minds. It is not for the sake of making a noise in their houses, as many of them say by way of an excuse. No! believe me, they know that pleasing entertainment arrests the attention of their customers from off the drink for the time being, and that is the chief reason for them not permitting it, and, from my own experience, I know it to be the case.

I remember another night while in a public-house. This was on a Saturday night, and the room I was in was quite full, both of men and women, and, of course, I was well known to the most of them. However, I was requested to sing them a song, or give them a recitation, which, of course, I consented to do on one condition, that I was paid for it, which the company agreed to do. So accordingly I sang "The Rattling Boy from Dublin," which was well received by the company. Then they proposed I should recite my Bannockburn poem, which I did, and after I had finished, and partaken of a little refreshment, the company made up for me a handsome collection. Then I began to think it was time for me to leave, as they seemed rather inclined to sing and enjoy themselves. However, when I got up to leave the company, I missed my stick. Lo and behold! it was gone from the place I had left it, and was nowhere to be seen by me or anyone else in the company. And while I was searching for it, and making a great fuss about it, one of the waiters chanced to come in with drink to the company, and he told me it had been taken away; for what purpose, my friends, if you know not, I will tell you; to make me leave the house, because I was getting too much money from the company, and the landlady guessed I would leave the house when I missed my stick, which was really the case.

I remember another Saturday night I was in the same public-house, and I was entertaining a number of gentlemen, and had received a second collection of money from them, and as soon as the landlady found out I was getting so much money, she rushed into the room and ordered me out at once, telling me to "hook it" out of here, and laid hold of me by the arm and showed me to the door.

Another case, I remember, happened to me in Perth; worse, in my opinion, than that. Well, my friends I chanced to be travelling at the time, and, being in very poor circumstances, I thought I would call at a public-house where I was a little acquainted with the landlord, and ask him if he would allow me to give an entertainment in one of his rooms, and I would feel obliged to him if he would be so kind. Well, however, he consented with a little flattery. Sometimes flattery does well; and in reference to flattery I will quote the beautiful lines of John Dryden the poet:—

"Flattery, like ice, our footing does betray,
Who can tread sure on the smooth slippery way?
Pleased with the fancy, we glide swiftly on,
And see the danger which we cannot shun."

The entertainment was to come off that night, and to commence at eight o'clock. So, my friends, I travelled around the city — God knows, tired, hungry, and footsore — inviting the people to come and hear me give my entertainment; and, of course, a great number of rich men and poor men came to hear me, and the room was filled by seven o'clock. But, remember, my dear friends, when I wanted to begin, the publican would not allow me until he had almost extracted every penny from the pockets of the company. And when he told me to begin, I remember I felt very reluctant to do so, for I knew I would get but a small recompense for my entertainment. And it just turned out to be as I expected. My dear friends, I only received eighteenpence for my entertainment from I daresay about sixty of a company. I ask of you, my dear readers, how much did the publican realise from the company that night by selling drink? In my opinion, the least he would have realised would be eighteen shillings or a pound. But, depend upon it, they will never take the advantage of me again.

My dear friends, I entreat of you all, for God's sake and for the furtherance of Christ's kingdom, to abstain from all kinds of intoxicating liquor, because seldom any good emanates from it. In the first place, if it was abolished, there would not be so much housebreaking, for this reason: When the burglar wants to break into a house, if he thinks he hasn't got enough courage to do so, he knows that if he takes a few glasses of either rum, whisky, or brandy, it will give him the courage to rob and kill honest disposed people. Yet the Government tolerates such a demon, I may call it, to be sold in society; to help burglars and thieves to rob and kill; also to help the seducer to seduce our daughters; and to help to fill our prisons, and our lunatic asylums, and our poorhouses.

Therefore, for these few sufficient reasons, I call upon
you, fathers and mothers, and the friends of Christianity,
and the friends of humanity,

To join each one, with heart and hand,
And help to banish the bane of society from our land
And trust in God, and worship Him,
And denounce the publicans, because they cause sin;
Therefore cease from strong drink,
And you will likely do well,
Then there's not so much danger of going to hell!

My dear friends, along with my experiences amongst
the publicans, I will relate to you a rather dangerous
adventure that happened to me some years ago, as follows. Being on travel in the parish of Liff, that is, I think,
about six miles from Dundee, and as I was very hard up
for money at the time, and being rather at a loss how to
get a little of that filthy lucre, as some people term it. But,
my dear readers, I never considered it to be either filthy or
bad. Money is most certainly the most useful commodity
in society that I know of. It is certainly good when not
abused; but, if abused, the fault rests with the abuser —
the money is good nevertheless. For my own part, I have
always found it to be one of my best friends. Well, being
near to a smithy at the time I refer to, I resolved to call on
the smith at the smithy and ask his permission to be allowed to give an entertainment from my own works in the
smithy that same night. And when I called on the smith
and asked his permission to give my entertainment, and
told him who I was, he granted me permission of the
smithy cheerfully to give my entertainment. So I went
from house to house in the district, inviting the people to

come to my entertainment, which was to commence at eight o'clock. Admission — adults, twopence each; children, one penny each. When it drew near to eight o'clock there was a very respectable audience gathered to hear me, and gave me a very hearty welcome and a patient hearing; and they all felt highly delighted with the entertainment I had given them, and many of them inviting me to hurry back again, and give them another entertainment. The proceeds, I remember, for the entertainment I gave amounted to four shillings and ninepence, which I was very thankful for. Well, my dear friends, after I had thanked the smith for the liberty of his smithy, and had left and had drawn near to Liff school-room, I heard the pattering of men's feet behind me, and an undefinable fear seized me. Having my umbrella with me I grasped it firmly, and waited patiently until three men came up to me near Liff school-room, and there they stood glaring at me as the serpent does before it leaps upon its prey. Then the man in the centre of the three whispered to his companions, and, as he did so, he threw out both his hands, with the intention, no doubt, of knocking me down, and, with the assistance of the other two, robbing me of the money I had realised from my entertainment. But when he threw out his arms to catch hold of me, as quick as lightning I struck him a blow across the legs with my umbrella, which made him leap backwards, and immediately they then went away round to the front of the school-master's house, close by the road side, and planted themselves there. And when I saw they were waiting for me to come that way as they expected, I resolved to make my escape from them the best way I could. But how? ah, that was the rub. However, I went round to the front of the school-master's house, and reviewed them in the distance, and,

the night being dark, the idea struck me if I could manage
to get away from their sight they would give up the chase,
and go home to Lochee without satisfying their evil inten-
tions. Well, my friends, the plan I adopted was by lower-
ing my body slowly downwards until my knees were
touching the ground, and, in that position, I remained for
a few seconds; then I threw myself flat on my face on the
road, and I remained in that way watching them in the
greatest fear imaginable. But, thank God, the plan I
adopted had the desired effect of saving me from being
robbed, or perhaps murdered. Then I thought it advisable
to go home by Birkhill, for fear of meeting the night
poachers or prowlers again. And when I arrived at Birkhill
I resolved to go home by passing through Lord Duncan's
woods. I considered it would be safer doing so than by going home the way the poachers had gone, and, just as I
made my entry into Lord Duncan's woods, I began to
sing—

Yea, though I walk in death's dark vale,
    Yet will I fear none ill,
For Thou art with me, and Thy rod
    And staff me comfort still.

So, my dear readers, I arrived safe home, and thanked
God for delivering me from the hands of evil-doers, as He
has done on all occasions.

Saving a Train

'Twas in the year of 1869, and on the 19th of November,
Which the people in Southern Germany will long remember,
The great rain-storm which for twenty hours did pour down,
That the rivers were overflowed and petty streams all around.

The rain fell in such torrents as had never been seen before,
That it seemed like a second deluge, the mighty
   torrents' roar,
At nine o'clock at night the storm did rage and moan,
When Carl Springel set out on his crutches all alone—

From the handsome little hut in which he dwelt,
With some food to his father, for whom he greatly felt,
Who was watching at the railway bridge,
Which was built upon a perpendicular rocky ridge.

The bridge was composed of iron and wooden blocks,
And crossed o'er the Devil's Gulch, an immense cleft
   of rocks,
Two hundred feet wide and one hundred and fifty feet deep,
And enough to make one's flesh to creep.

Far beneath the bridge a mountain-stream did boil and
   rumble,
And on that night did madly toss and tumble;
Oh! it must have been an awful sight
To see the great cataract falling from such a height.

It was the duty of Carl's father to watch the bridge on
   stormy nights,
And warn the on-coming trains of danger with the red lights;
So, on this stormy night, the boy Carl hobbled along
Slowly and fearlessly upon his crutches, because he
   wasn't strong.

He struggled on manfully with all his might
Through the fearful darkness of the night,

And half-blinded by the heavy rain,
But still resolved the bridge to gain.

But, when within one hundred yards of the bridge, it gave
   way with an awful crash,
And fell into the roaring flood below, and made a
   fearful splash,
Which rose high above the din of the storm,
The like brave Carl never heard since he was born.

Then father! father! cried Carl in his loudest tone,
Father! father! he shouted again in very pitiful moans;
But no answering voice did reply,
Which caused him to heave a deep-fetched sigh.

And now to brave Carl the truth was clear
That he had lost his father dear,
And he cried, My poor father's lost, and cannot be found,
He's gone down with the bridge, and has been drowned.

But he resolves to save the on-coming train,
So every nerve and muscle he does strain,
And he trudges along dauntlessly on his crutches,
And tenaciously to them he clutches.

And just in time he reaches his father's car
To save the on-coming train from afar,
So he seizes the red light, and swings it round,
And cried with all his might, The bridge is down! The bridge
   is down!

So forward his father's car he drives,
Determined to save the passengers' lives,
Struggling hard with might and main,
Hoping his struggle won't prove in vain.

So on comes the iron-horse snorting and rumbling,
And the mountain-torrent at the bridge kept roaring
   and tumbling;
While brave Carl keeps shouting, The bridge is down!
   The bridge is down!
He cried with a pitiful wail and sound.

But, thank heaven, the engine-driver sees the red light
That Carl keeps swinging round his head with all his might;
But bang! bang! goes the engine with a terrible crash,
And the car is dashed all to smash.

But the breaking of the car stops the train,
And poor Carl's struggle is not in vain;
But, poor soul, he was found stark dead,
Crushed and mangled from foot to head!

And the passengers were all loud in Carl's praise,
And from the cold wet ground they did him raise,
And tears for brave Carl fell silently around,
Because he had saved two hundred passengers from being
   drowned.

In a quiet village cemetery he now sleeps among the
   silent dead,
In the south of Germany, with a tombstone at his head,
Erected by the passengers he saved in the train,
And which to his memory will long remain.

The Rattling Boy
from Dublin

I'm a rattling boy from Dublin Town,
I courted a girl called Biddy Brown,
Her eyes they were as black as sloes,
She had black hair and an aquiline nose.

Chorus—
Whack fal de da, fal de darelido,
Whack fal de da, fal de darelay,
Whack fal de da, fal de darelido,
Whack fal de da, fal de darelay.

One night I met her with another lad,
Says I, Biddy, I've caught you, by dad;
I never thought you were half so bad
As to be going about with another lad.

Chorus.

Says I, Biddy, this will never do,
For to-night you've prov'd to me untrue,
So do not make a hullaballoo,
For I will bid farewell to you.

Chorus.

Says Barney Magee, she is my lass,
And the man that says no, he is an ass,
So come away, and I'll give you a glass,
Och, sure you can get another lass.

Chorus.

Says I, To the devil with your glass,
You have taken from me my darling lass,
And if you look angry, or offer to frown,
With my darling shillelah I'll knock you down.

Chorus.

Says Barney Magee unto me,
By the hokey I love Biddy Brown,
And before I'll give her up to thee,
One or both of us will go down.

Chorus.

So, with my darling shillelah, I gave him a whack,
Which left him lying on his back,
Saying, botheration to you and Biddy Brown,—
For I'm the rattling boy from Dublin town.

Chorus.

So a policeman chanced to come up at the time,
And he asked of me the cause of the shine,
Says I, he threatened to knock me down
When I challenged him for walking with my Biddy Brown.

Chorus.

So the policeman took Barney Magee to jail,
Which made him shout and bewail
That ever he met with Biddy Brown,
The greatest deceiver in Dublin town.

Chorus.

So I bade farewell to Biddy Brown,
The greatest jilter in Dublin town,
Because she proved untrue to me,
And was going about with Barney Magee.

Chorus.

Annie Marshall
the Foundling

Annie Marshall was a foundling, and lived in Downderry,
And was trained up by a coast-guardsman, kind-hearted
    and merry,
And he loved Annie Marshall as dear as his life,
And he resolved to make her his own loving wife.

The night was tempestuous, most terrific, and pitch dark,
When Matthew Pengelly rescued Annie Marshall from an
    ill-fated barque,
But her parents were engulfed in the briny deep,
Which caused poor Annie at times to sigh and weep.

One day Matthew asked Annie if she would be his wife,
And Annie replied, I never thought of it in all my life;
Yes, my wife, Annie, replied Matthew, hold hard a bit,
Remember, Annie, I've watched you grow up, and consider
   you most fit.

Poor Annie did not speak, she remained quite mute,
And with agitation she trembled from head to foot,
The poor girl was in a dilemma, she knew not what to say,
And owing to Matthew training her, she couldn't say
   him nay.

Oh! Matthew, I'm afraid I would not make you a good wife,
And in that respect there would be too much strife,
And the thought thereof, believe me, makes me feel ill,
Because I'm unfit to be thy wife, Matthew, faltered the
   poor girl.

Time will prove that, dear Annie, but why are you so calm?
Then Annie put her hand shyly into Matthew's brown palm
Just then the flashing lightning played upon Annie's face,
And the loud thunder drowned Matthew's words as Annie
   left the place.

But Matthew looked after her as she went home straightway.
And his old heart felt light and gay,
As he looked forward for his coming marriage day,
Because he knew that Annie Marshall couldn't say him nay.

Then the sky drew dark, and the sea lashed itself into foam,
But he heeded it not as he sat there alone,
Till the sound of a gun came booming o'er the sea,
Then Matthew had to attend to his duty immediately.

A ship, he muttered, Lord, help them! and coming right in by
   the sound,
And in a few minutes she will run aground.
And the vessel was dashed against the rocks with her
   helpless crew,
Then in hot haste for assistance Matthew instantly flew.

Then Matthew returned with a few men all willing to lend
  their aid,
But amongst them all Matthew seemed the least afraid;
Then an old man cried, Save my boy, for his mother's sake,
Oh! Matthew, try and save him, or my heart will break!

I will, Heaven helping me, Matthew said solemnly,
Come, bear a hand, mates, and lower me over the
  cliff quietly;
Then Matthew was lowered with ropes into what seemed a
  watery grave,
At the risk of his own life, old Jonathan Bately's son to save.

So Matthew Pengelly saved Jonathan Bately's son,
And the old man thanked God and Matthew for what
  he had done,
And the mother's heart was full of gratitude and joy,
For the restoration of her darling boy.

So Matthew resolved to marry Annie Marshall,
But first he'd go to sea whatever did befall,
To earn a few pounds to make the marriage more grand,
So he joined a whaling vessel and went to Greenland.

And while Matthew was away at Greenland,
David Bately wanted to marry Annie Marshall right off hand,
But Annie refused to marry David Bately,
So in anger David Bately went another voyage to sea.

A few nights after David Bately had gone to sea,
Annie's thoughts reverted to Matthew Pengelly,
And as she sat in the Downderry station watching the
  boiling waves below,
The wind blew a terrific gale, which filled her heart with woe.

And as she sat there the big waves did loudly roar,
When a man cried, Help! help! there's a corpse washed
  ashore;
Then Annie rushed madly to the little beach,
And when she saw the corpse she gave a loud screech.

So there is but little more to tell of this sad history,
Only that Annie Marshall mourned long for Matthew
    Pengelly,
Who had floated home to be buried amongst his own kin,
But, alas! the rest of the crew were buried in the sea,
    save him.

Baldovan

The scenery of Baldovan
Is most lovely to see,
Near by Dighty Water,
Not far from Dundee.

'Tis health for any one
To be walking there,
O'er the green swards of Baldovan,
And in the forests fair.

There the blackbird and the mavis
Together merrily do sing
In the forest of Baldovan,
Making the woodlands to ring.

'Tis delightful to hear them
On a fine summer day,
Carolling their cheerful notes
So blythe and so gay.

Then there's the little loch near by,
Whereon can be seen every day
Numerous wild ducks swimming
And quacking in their innocent play.

Robert Burns

Immortal Robert Burns of Ayr,
There's but few poets can with you compare;
Some of your poems and songs are very fine:
"To Mary in Heaven" is most sublime;
And then again in your "Cottar's Saturday Night,"
Your genius there does shine most bright,
As pure as the dewdrops of night.

Your "Tam o' Shanter" is very fine,
Both funny, racy, and divine,
From John o' Groats to Dumfries
All critics consider it to be a masterpiece,
And, also, you have said the same,
Therefore they are not to blame.

And in my own opinion both you and they are right,
For your genius there does sparkle bright,
Which I most solemnly declare
To thee, Immortal Bard of Ayr!

Your "Banks and Braes of Bonnie Doon"
Is sweet and melodious in its tune,
And the poetry is moral and sublime,
And in my opinion nothing can be more fine.

Your "Scots wha hae wi' Wallace bled"
Is most beautiful to hear sung or read;
For your genius there does shine as bright,
Like unto the stars of night. . . .

Immortal Bard of Ayr! I must conclude my muse
To speak in praise of thee does not refuse,
For you were a mighty poet, few could with you compare,
And also an honour to Scotland, for your genius it is rare.

The Sorrows of the Blind

Pity the sorrows of the poor blind,
For they can but little comfort find;
As they walk along the street,
They know not where to put their feet.
They are deprived of that earthly joy
Of seeing either man, woman, or boy;
Sad and lonely through the world they go,
Not knowing a friend from a foe:
Nor the difference betwixt day and night,
For the want of their eyesight;
The blind mother cannot see her darling boy,
That was once her soul's joy.
By day and night,
Since she lost her precious sight;
To her the world seems dark and drear,
And she can find no comfort here.
She once found pleasure in reading books,
But now pale and careworn are her looks.
Since she has lost her eyesight,
Everything seems wrong and nothing right.

The face of nature, with all its beauties and livery green,
Appears to the blind just like a dream.
All things beautiful have vanished from their sight,
Which were once their heart's delight.
The blind father cannot see his beautiful child, nor wife,
That was once the joy of his life;
That he was wont to see at morn and night,
When he had his eyesight.
All comfort has vanished from him now,
And a dejected look hangs on his brow.

Kind Christians all, both great and small,
Pity the sorrows of the blind,
They can but little comfort find;
Therefore we ought to be content with our lot,

And for the eyesight we have got,
And pray to God both day and night
To preserve our eyesight;
To be always willing to help the blind in their distress,
And the Lord will surely bless
And guard us by night and day,
And remember us at the judgment day.

An Ode to the Queen

On Her Jubilee Year

Sound drums and trumpets, far and near!
And let all Queen Victoria's subjects loudly cheer!
And show by their actions that her they revere,
Because she's served them faithfully fifty long year!

All hail to the Empress of India and Great Britain's Queen!
Long may she live happy and serene!
And as this is now her Jubilee year,
I hope her subjects will show their loyalty without fear.

Therefore let all her subjects rejoice and sing,
Until they make the welkin ring;
And let young and old on this her Jubilee be glad,
And cry, "Long Live our Queen!" and don't be sad.

She has been a good Queen, which no one dare gainsay,
And I hope God will protect her for many a day;
May He enable her a few more years to reign,
And let all her lieges say — Amen!

Let all hatred towards her be thrown aside
All o'er dominions broad and wide;

And let all her subjects bear in mind,
By God kings and queens are put in trust o'er mankind.

Therefore rejoice and be glad on her Jubilee day,
And try and make the heart of our Queen feel gay;
Oh! try and make her happy in country and town,
And not with Shakspeare say, "uneasy lies the head that
   wears a crown."

And as this is her first Jubilee year,
And will be her last, I rather fear;
Therefore, sound drums and trumpets cheerfully,
Until the echoes are heard o'er land and sea.

And let the innocent voices of the children at home or abroad
Ascend with cheerful shouts to the throne of God;
And sing aloud, "God Save our Gracious Queen!"
Because a good and charitable Sovereign she has been.

Therefore, ye sons of Great Britain, come join with me,
And welcome in our noble Queen's Jubilee;
Because she has been a faithful Queen, ye must confess,
There hasn't been her equal since the days of Queen Bess.

Therefore let all her lieges shout and cheer,
"God Save our Gracious Queen!" for many a year;
Let such be the cry in the peasant's cot, the hall,
With stentorian voices, as loud as they can bawl.

And let bonfires be kindled on every hill,
And her subjects dance around them at their freewill;
And try to drive dull care away
By singing and rejoicing on the Queen's Jubilee day.

May God protect her for many a day,
At home or abroad when she's far away;
Long may she be spared o'er her subjects to reign,
And let each and all with one voice say — Amen!

Victoria is a good Queen, which all her subjects know,
And for that may God protect her from every foe;
May He be as a hedge around her, as He's been all along,
And let her live and die in peace — is the end of my song.

The Nithsdale Widow and Her Son

'Twas in the year of 1746, on a fine summer afternoon,
When trees and flowers were in full bloom,
That widow Riddel sat knitting stockings on a little
    rustic seat,
Which her only son had made for her, which was very neat.
The cottage she lived in was in the wilds of Nithsdale,
Where many a poor soul had cause to bewail
The loss of their shealings, that were burned to the ground,
By a party of fierce British dragoons that chanced to
    come round.

While widow Riddel sat in her garden she heard an
    unusual sound,
And near by was her son putting some seeds into the
    ground,
And as she happened to look down into the little
    strath below
She espied a party of dragoons coming towards her
    very slow.

And hearing of the cruelties committed by them, she shook
    with fear.
And she cried to her son, "Jamie, thae sodgers are
    coming here!"
While the poor old widow's heart with fear was panting,
And she cried, "Mercy on us, Jamie, what can they
    be wanting?"

Next minute the dragoons were in front of the cottage door,
When one of them dismounted, and loudly did roar,
"Is there any rebels, old woman, skulking hereabouts."
"Oh, no, Sir, no! believe my word without any doubts."
"Well, so much the better, my good woman, for you
    and them;
But, old girl, let's have something to eat, me, and my men":
"Blithely, sir, blithely! ye're welcome to what I hae,"
When she bustled into the cottage without delay.
And she brought out oaten cakes, sweet milk, and cheese,
Which the soldiers devoured greedily at their ease,
And of which they made a hearty meal,
But, for such kind treatment, ungrateful they did feel.

Then one of the soldiers asked her how she got her living:
She replied, "God unto her was always giving;
And wi' the bit garden, alang wi' the bit coo,
And wi' what the laddie can earn we are sincerely thankfu'."

To this pitiful detail of her circumstances the villain made
    no reply,
But drew a pistol from his holster, and cried, "Your cow
    must die!"
Then riding up to the poor cow, discharged it through
    her head,
When the innocent animal instantly feel down dead.

Not satisfied with this the merciless ruffian leaped the little
    garden wall,
And with his horse trod down everything, the poor
    widow's all,
Then having finished this barbarous act of direst cruelty,
The monster rejoined his comrades shouting right merrily:

"There, you old devil, that's what you really deserve,
For you and your rascally rebels ought to starve";
Then the party rode off, laughing at the mischief that
    was done,
Leaving the poor widow to mourn and her only son.

When the widow found herself deprived of her all,
She wrung her hands in despair, and on God did call,

Then rushed into the cottage and flung herself on her bed,
And, with sorrow, in a few days she was dead.
And during her illness, her poor boy never left her bedside,
There he remained, night and day, his mother's wants to
　　provide,
And make her forget the misfortunes that had befallen them,
All through that villainous and hard-hearted party of men.

On the fourth day her son followed her remains to the grave.
And during the burial service he most manfully did behave,
And when the body was laid in the grave, from tears he
　　could not refrain,
But instantly fled from that desolated place, and never
　　returned again.

Thirteen years after this the famous battle of Minden
　　was fought
By Prince Ferdinand against the French, who brought them
　　to nought;
And there was a large body of British horse, under Lord
　　George Sackville,
And strange! the widow's son was at the battle all the while.

And on the evening after the battle there were assembled in
　　a tavern
A party of British dragoons, loudly boasting and swearing,
When one of them swore he had done more than any
　　of them—
A much more meritorious action—which he defied them
　　to condemn.

"What was that, Tam, what was that, Tam?" shouted his
　　companions at once.
"Tell us, Tam; tell us, Tam, was that while in France?"
"No!" he cried, "it was starving an old witch, while in
　　Nithsdale,
By shooting her cow and riding down her greens, that is
　　the tale."
"And don't you repent it?" exclaimed a young soldier, present.
"Repent what?" cried the braggart; "No! I feel quite content."
"Then, villain!" cried the youth, unsheathing his sword,
"That woman was my mother, so not another word!

"So draw, and defend yourself, without more delay,
For I swear you shall not live another day!"
Then the villain sprang to his feet, and a combat ensued,
But in three passes he was entirely subdued.

Young Riddel afterwards rose to be a captain
In the British service, and gained a very good name
For being a daring soldier, wherever he went,
And as for killing the ruffian dragoon he never did repent.

General Gordon,
the Hero of Khartoum

Alas! now o'er the civilised world there hangs a gloom
For brave General Gordon, that was killed in Khartoum;
He was a Christian hero, and a soldier of the Cross,
And to England his death will be a very great loss.

He was very cool in temper, generous and brave,
The friend of the poor, the sick, and the slave;
And many a poor boy he did educate,
And laboured hard to do so early and late.

He was a man that did not care for worldly gear,
Because the living and true God he did fear;
And the hearts of the poor he liked to cheer,
And by his companions in arms he was loved most dear.

He always took the Bible for his guide,
And he liked little boys to walk by his side;
He preferred their company more so than men,
Because he knew there was less guile in them.

And in his conversation he was modest and plain,
Denouncing all pleasures he considered sinful and vain,

And in battle he carried no weapon but a small cane,
Whilst the bullets fell around him like a shower of rain.

He burnt the debtors' books that were imprisoned in
  Khartoum,
And freed them from a dismal prison gloom,
Those that were imprisoned for debt they couldn't pay,
And sent them rejoicing on their way.

While engaged in the Russian war, in the midst of the fight,
He stood upon a rising ground and viewed them left and
right,
But for their shot and shell he didn't care a jot,
While the officers cried, Gordon, come down, or else you'll
  be shot.

His cane was christened by the soldiers Gordon's wand of
  victory,
And when he waved it the soldiers' hearts were filled
  with glee,
While with voice and gesture he encouraged them in the
  strife,
And he himself appeared to possess a charmed life.

Once when leading a storming party the soldiers drew back,
But he quickly observed that courage they did lack,
Then he calmly lighted a cigar, and turned cheerfully round,
And the soldiers rushed boldly on with a bound.

And they carried the position without delay,
And the Chinese rebels soon gave way,
Because God was with him during the day,
And with those that trust Him for ever and aye.

He was always willing to conduct meetings for the poor,
Also meat and clothing for them he tried to procure,
And he always had little humorous speeches at command,
And to hear him deliver them it must have been grand.

In military life his equal couldn't be found,
No! if you were to search the wide world around,

And 'tis pitiful to think he has met with such a doom
by a base *traitor knave* while in Khartoum.

Yes, the black-hearted traitor opened the gates of Khartoum,
And through that the Christian hero has met his doom,
For when the gates were opened the Arabs rushed madly in,
And foully murdered him while they laughingly did grin.

But he defended himself nobly with axe and sword in hand,
But, alas! he was soon overpowered by that savage band,
And his body received a hundred spear wounds and more,
While his murderers exultingly did loudly shriek and roar.

But heaven's will, 'tis said, must be done,
And according to his own opinion his time was come;
but I hope he is now in heaven reaping his reward.
Although his fate on earth was really very hard.

I hope the people will his memory revere,
And take an example from him, and worship God in fear,
And never be too fond of worldly gear,
And walk in General Gordon's footsteps, while they are here.

The Death of
the Old Mendicant

There was a rich old gentleman
Lived on a lonely moor in Switzerland,
And he was very hard to the wandering poor,
'Tis said he never lodged nor served them at his door.

'Twas on a stormy night, and Boreas blew a bitter blast,
And the snowflakes they fell thick and fast,
When a poor old mendicant, tired and footsore,

Who had travelled that day fifteen miles and more,
Knocked loudly at the rich man's door.

The rich man was in his parlour counting his gold,
And he ran to the door to see who was so bold,
And there he saw the mendicant shivering with the cold.

Then the mendicant unto him said,
My dear sir, be not afraid,
Pray give me lodgings for the night,
And heaven will your love requite;
Have pity on me, for I am tired and footsore,
I have travelled fifteen miles to-day and more.

Begone! you vagabond, from my door!
I never give lodgings to the poor;
So be off, take to your heels and run,
Or else I'll shoot you with my gun!
Now do not think I'm making fun;
Do you hear, old beggar, what I say?
Now be quick! and go away.

Have mercy, sir I cannot go,
For I shall perish in the snow;
Oh! for heaven's sake, be not so hard
And God will your love reward.

My limbs are tired, I cannot go away,
Oh! be so kind as let me stay.
'Twas vain! the rich man said, I shan't,
And shut his door on the mendicant,
And said, That is the way I'll serve the poor
While I live on this lonely moor.

Then the old mendicant did go away,
And, murmuring to himself, did say,
Oh, woe's me that ever I was born!
Oh, God, protect me from the storm!
My feeble limbs refuse to go,
And my poor heart does break with woe.

Then he lay down and died among the snow.
He was found by the rich man's shepherd next day,
While he was searching for sheep that had gone astray;
And he was struck with fear and woe
To see the body lying dead among the snow.

So the shepherd ran home and told his master
About the very sad disaster;
That he had found a dead body in the snow,
But whose it was he did not know.

Then the rich man ordered the body to be brought to his
    house
And to be instantly dressed by his loving spouse,
For his conscience smote him with fear and woe,
When he heard of the old mendicant being found dead in
    the snow.

So the poor old mendicant was buried without delay
In a very respectable way;
And from that very day the rich man was kind to the poor
And never turned any one away from his door.

Bill Bowls the Sailor

'Twas about the beginning of the present century,
Bill Bowls was pressed, and sent to sea;
And conveyed on board the "Waterwitch" without delay,
Scarce getting time to bid farewell to the villagers of Fairway.

And once on board the "Waterwitch," he resolved to do
    his duty,
And God willing, he'd marry Nelly Blyth, the village beauty;
And he'd fight for Old England, like a jolly British tar,
But he'd think of Nelly Blyth during the war.

The poor fellow little imagined what he had to go through,
But in all his trials at sea, he never did rue;
No; the brave tar became reconciled to his fate,
And he felt proud of his commander, Captain Ward
the great.

And on board the "Waterwitch" was Tom Riggles, his old
comrade,
And with such a one as Tom Riggles he seldom felt afraid,
Because the stories they told on board made the time
fly away,
And made the hearts of their messmates feel light and gay.

'Twas on a sunny morning, and clear to the view,
Captain Ward the close attention of his men he drew:
Look! he cried, there's two Frenchmen of war on our right,
Therefore, prepare my men immediately to commence
the fight.

Then the "Waterwitch" was steered to the ship most near,
While every man resolved to sell his life most dear;
But the French commander, disinclined to commence
the fight,
Ordered his men to put on a press of canvas and take to
flight.

But Captain Ward quickly gave the order to fire,
Then Bill Bowls cried, Now we'll get fighting to our heart's
desire!
And for an hour and more a running fight was maintained,
Until the two ships of the enemy near upon the "Waterwitch"
gained.

Captain Ward walked the deck with a firm tread,
When a shot from the enemy pierced the ship's side above
his head;
And with a splinter Bill Bowls was wounded on the left arm,
And he cried, Death to the frog-eaters! they have done me
little harm.

Then Captain Ward cried, Fear not, we will win the day,
Now, courage my men, pour in broadsides without delay;

Then they sailed round the "St. Denis" and the "Gloire,"
And in at their cabin windows they poured a deadly fire.

The effect on the two ships was fearful to behold,
But still the Frenchmen stuck to their guns with courage,
    be it told;
And the crash and din of artillery was deafening to the ear,
And the cries of the wounded men on deck were pitiful
    to hear.

Then Captain Ward to his men did say,
We must board these French ships without dismay;
Then he seized his cutlass, as he fearlessly spoke,
And jumped on board the "St. Denis" in the midst of
    the smoke.

Then Bill Bowls and Tom Riggles quickly followed him,
Then hand to hand the battle in earnest did begin;
And the men sprang upon their foes and beat them back,
And they hauled down their colours, and hoisted the
    Union Jack.

But the men on board the "St. Denis" fought desperately
    hard,
But, alas! as the "St. Denis" was captured, a ball struck
    Captain Ward
Right on the forehead, and he fell dead with a groan,
And for the death of Captain Ward the sailors did cry
    and moan.

Then the first lieutenant, who was standing by,
Loudly to the men did cry:
Come men, and carry your noble commander to his cabin
    below,
But there is one consolation, we have beaten the foe.

And thus fell Captain Ward in the prime of his life,
And I hope he is now in the better land, free from strife:
But, alas! 'tis sad to think he was buried in the mighty deep,
Where too many of our brave seamen do silently sleep.

The "St. Denis" and the "Gloire" were towed to Gibraltar,
    the nearest port,
But by capturing of them, they felt but little sport,
Because, for the loss of Captain Ward, the men felt
    woebegone,
Because in bravery, they said, he was next to Admiral
    Nelson.

Burning of the Exeter Theatre

'Twas in the year of 1887, which many people will long
    remember,
The burning of the Theatre at Exeter on the 5th of
    September,
Alas! that ever-to-be-remembered and unlucky night,
When one hundred and fifty lost their lives, a most
    agonising sight.

The play on this night was called "Romany Rye,"
And at act four, scene third, Fire! Fire! was the cry;
And all in a moment flames were seen issuing from
    the stage,
Then the women screamed frantically, like wild beasts in
    a cage.

Then a panic ensued, and each one felt dismayed,
And from the burning building a rush was made;
And soon the theatre was filled with a blinding smoke,
So that the people their way out had to grope.

The shrieks of those trying to escape were fearful to hear,
Especially the cries of those who had lost their friends
    most dear;

Oh, the scene was most painful in the London Inn Square,
To see them wringing their hands and tearing their hair!

And as the flames spread, great havoc they did make,
And the poor souls fought heroically in trying to make their
  escape;
Oh, it was horrible to see men and women trying to reach
  the door!
But in many cases death claimed the victory, and their
  struggles were o'er.

Alas! 'twas pitiful the shrieks of the audience to hear,
Especially as the flames to them drew near;
Because on every face were depicted despair and woe,
And many of them jumped from the windows into the street
  below.

The crushed and charred bodies were carried into London
  Hotel yard,
And to alleviate their sufferings the doctors tried hard;
But, alas! their attendance on many was thrown away,
But those that survived were conveyed to Exeter Hospital
  without delay.

And all those that had their wounds dressed proceeded
  home,
Accompanied by their friends, and making a loud moan;
While the faces and necks of others were sickening to
  behold,
Enough to chill one's blood, and make the heart turn cold.

Alas! words fail to describe the desolation,
And in many homes it will cause great lamentation;
Because human remains are beyond all identification,
Which will cause the relatives of the sufferers to be in great
  tribulation.

Oh, Heaven! it must have been an awful sight,
To see the poor souls struggling hard with all their might,
Fighting hard their lives to save,
While many in the smoke and burning flame did madly rave!

It was the most sickening sight that ever anybody saw,
Human remains, beyond recognition, covered with a heap
of straw;
And here and there a body might be seen, and a maimed
hand,
Oh, such a sight, that the most hard-hearted person could
hardly withstand!

The number of the people in the theatre was between seven
and eight thousand,
But, alas! one hundred and fifty by the fire have been
found dead;
And the most lives were lost on the stairs leading from the
gallery,
And these were roasted to death, which was sickening
to see.

The funerals were conducted at the expense of the local
authority,
And two hours and more elapsed at the mournful ceremony;
And at one grave there were two thousand people, a very
great crowd,
And most of the men were bareheaded and weeping aloud.

Alas! many poor children have been bereft of their fathers
and mothers,
Who will be sorely missed by little sisters and brothers;
But, alas! unto them they can ne'er return again,
Therefore the poor little innocents must weep for them
in vain.

I hope all kind Christian souls will help the friends of
the dead,
Especially those that have lost the winners of their bread;
And if they do, God surely will them bless,
Because pure Christianity is to help the widows and orphans
in distress.

I am very glad to see Henry Irving has sent a hundred
pounds,
And I hope his brother actors will subscribe their mite all
round;

And if they do it will add honour to their name,
Because whatever is given towards a good cause they will
    it regain.

Loch Leven

Beautiful Loch Leven, near by Kinross,
For a good day's fishing the angler is seldom at a loss,
For the loch it abounds with pike and trout,
Which can be had for the catching without any doubt;
And the scenery around it is most beautiful to be seen,
Especially the Castle, wherein was imprisoned Scotland's
    ill-starred Queen.

Then there's the lofty Lomond Hills on the eastern side,
And the loch is long, very deep, and wide;
Then on the southern side there's Benarty's rugged hills,
And from the tops can be seen the village of Kinross with its
    spinning mills.

The big house of Kinross is very handsome to be seen,
With its beautiful grounds around it, and lime trees so green
And 'tis a magnificent sight to see, on a fine summer
    afternoon,
The bees extracting honey from the leaves when in full
bloom.

There the tourist can enjoy himself and while away
    the hours,
Underneath the lime trees shady bowers,
And listen to the humming of the busy bees,
While they are busy gathering honey from the lime trees.

Then there's the old burying ground near by Kinross,
And the dead that lie there turned into dusty dross,
And the gravestones are all in a state of decay,
And the old wall around it is mouldering away.

The Burial of the Rev. George Gilfillan

On the Gilfillan burial day,
In the Hill o' Balgay,
It was a most solemn sight to see,
Not fewer than thirty thousand people assembled in Dundee,
All watching the funeral procession of Gilfallan that day,
That death had suddenly taken away,
And was going to be buried in the Hill o' Balgay.

There were about three thousand people in the procession
    alone,
And many were shedding tears, and several did moan,
And their bosoms heaved with pain,
Because they knew they would never look upon his
    like again.

There could not be fewer than fifty carriages in the
    procession that day,
And gentlemen in some of them that had come from
    far away,
And in whispers some of them did say,
As the hearse bore the precious corpse away,
Along the Nethergate that day.

I'm sure he will be greatly missed by the poor,
For he never turned them empty-handed away from his door;
And to assist them in distress it didn't give him pain,
And I'm sure the poor will never look upon his like again.

On the Gilfillan burial day, in the Hill o' Balgay,
There was a body of policemen marshalled in grand array,
And marched in front of the procession all the way;
Also the relatives and friends of the deceas'd,
Whom I hope from all sorrows has been releas'd,
And whose soul I hope to heaven has fled away,
To sing with saints above for ever and aye.

The Provost, Magistrates, and Town Council were in the
    procession that day;
Also Mrs Gilfillan, who cried and sobbed all the way
For her kind husband, that was always affable and gay,
Which she will remember until her dying day.

When the procession arrived in the Hill o' Balgay,
The people were almost as hush as death, and many of them
    did say—
As long as we live we'll remember the day
That the great Gilfillan was buried in the Hill o' Balgay.

When the body of the great Gilfillan was lowered into
    the grave,
'Twas then the people's hearts with sorrow did heave;
And with tearful eyes and bated breath,
Mrs Gilfillan lamented her loving husband's death.

Then she dropped a ringlet of immortelles into his grave,
Then took one last fond look, and in sorrow did leave;
And all the people left with sad hearts that day,
And that ended the Gilfillan burial in the Hill o' Balgay.

Descriptive Jottings of London

As I stood upon London Bridge and viewed the mighty
    throng
Of thousands of people in cabs and 'busses rapidly
    whirling along,
All furiously driving to and fro,
Up one street and down another as quick as they could go:

Then I was struck with the discordant sounds of human
    voices there,
Which seemed to me like wild geese cackling in the air:
And the river Thames is a most beautiful sight,
To see the steamers sailing upon it by day and by night.

And the Tower of London is most gloomy to behold,
And the crown of England lies there, begemmed with
    precious stones and gold;
King Henry the Sixth was murdered there by the Duke
    of Glo'ster,
And when he killed him with his sword he called him
    an imposter.

St. Paul's Cathedral is the finest building that ever I did see,
There's no building can surpass it in the city of Dundee,
Because it's magnificent to behold,
With its beautiful dome and spire glittering like gold.

And as for Nelson's Monument that stands in Trafalgar
    Square,
It is a most stately monument I most solemnly declare,
And towering defiantly very high,
Which arrests strangers' attention while passing by.

Then there's two beautiful water-fountains spouting up
    very high,
Where the weary traveller can drink when he feels dry;
And at the foot of the monument there's three bronze lions
    in grand array,
Enough to make the stranger's heart throb with dismay.

Then there's Mr Spurgeon, a great preacher, which no one
    dare gainsay,
I went to hear him preach on the Sabbath-day,
And he made my heart feel light and gay,
When I heard him preach and pray.

And the Tabernacle was crowded from ceiling to floor,
And many were standing outside the door;
He is an eloquent preacher I honestly declare,
And I was struck with admiration as on him I did stare.

Then there's Petticoat Lane I venture to say,
It's a wonderful place on the Sabbath-day;
There wearing-apparel can be bought to suit the young
    or old.
For the ready cash, silver, coppers, or gold.

Oh! mighty city of London! you are wonderful to see,
And thy beauties no doubt fill the tourist's heart with glee;
But during my short stay, and while wandering there,
Mr Spurgeon was the only man I heard speaking proper
    English I do declare.

Jenny Carrister, the Heroine of Lucknow-Mine

A heroic story I will unfold,
Concerning Jenny Carrister, a heroine bold,
Who lived in Australia, at a gold mine called Lucknow,
And Jenny was beloved by the miners, somehow.

Jenny was the only daughter of the old lady who owned the
    mine—
And Jenny would come of an evening, like a gleam of
    sunshine,
And by the presence of her bright face and cheery voice,
She made the hearts of the unlucky diggers rejoice.

There was no pride about her, and day after day,
She walked with her young brother, who was always gay,
A beautiful boy he was, about thirteen years old,
And Jenny and her brother by the miners were greatly
    extolled.

Old Mrs Carrister was every inch a lady in her way,
Because she never pressed any of the miners that weren't
    able to pay
For the liberty of working the gold-field,
Which was thirty pounds per week for whatever it might
    yield.

It was in the early part of the year 1871,
That Jack Allingford, a miner, hit on a plan,
That in the mine, with powder, he'd loosen the granite-
    bound face,
So he selected, as he thought, a most suitable place.

And when all his arrangements had been made,
He was lowered down by a miner that felt a little afraid,
But most fortunately Jenny Carrister came up at the time,
Just as Jack Allingford was lowered into the mine.

Then she asked the man at the windlass if he'd had any luck,
But he picked up a piece of candle and then a match
    he struck;
Then Jenny asked the miner, What is that for?
And he replied to blast the mine, which I fear and abhor.

Then with a piece of rope he lowered the candle and
    matches into the mine,
While brave Jenny watched the action all the time;
And as the man continued to turn round the windlass handle,
Jenny asked him, Isn't it dangerous to lower the matches and
    candle?

Then the man replied, I hope there's no danger, Jenny,
    my lass,
But whatsoever God has ordained will come to pass;
And just as he said so the windlass handle swung round,
And struck him on the forehead, and he fell to the ground.

And when Jenny saw the blood streaming from the fallen
    man's head,
She rushed to the mouth of the shaft without any dread,
And Jenny called loudly, but received no reply,
So to her brother standing near by she heaved a deep sigh.

Telling him to run for assistance, while she swung herself on
    to the hand-rope,
Resolved to save Jack Allingford's life as she earnestly did
    hope;
And as she proceeded down the shaft at a quick pace,
The brave heroine knew that death was staring her in
    the face.

And the rope was burning her hands as she descended,
But she thought if she saved Jack her task would be ended;
And when she reached the bottom of the mine she did not
    hesitate,
But bounding towards Jack Allingford, who was lying
    seemingly inanimate.

And as she approached his body the hissing fuse burst
    upon her ears,
But still the noble girl no danger fears;
While the hissing of the fuse was like an engine grinding
    upon her brain,
Still she resolved to save Jack while life in her body did
    remain.

She noticed a small jet of smoke issuing from a hole near
    his head,
And if he'd lain a few seconds longer there he'd been
    killed dead,
But God had sent an angel to his rescue,
For seizing him by the arms his body to the air shaft
    she drew.

It was a supernatural effort, but she succeeded at last,
And Jenny thanked God when the danger was past,
But at the same instant the silence was broke·
By a loud explosion, which soon filled the mine with smoke.

But, oh, God be thanked! the greatest danger was past,
But when Jenny saw Jack Allingford, she stood aghast,
Because the blood was issuing from his nose and ears,
And as Jenny viewed his wounds she shed many tears.

But heroic Jenny was not one of the fainting sort,
For immediately to the mouth of the mine she did resort,
And she called loudly for help, the noble lass,
And her cry was answered by voices above at the windlass.

So there were plenty to volunteer their services below,
And the rope was attached to the windlass, and down they
    did go,
And Jack Allingford and Jenny were raised to the top,
While Jenny, noble soul, with exhaustion was like to drop.

And when the miners saw her safe above there was a burst
    of applause,
Because she had rescued Jack Allingford from death's jaws;
So all ye that read or hear this story, I have but to say,
That Jenny Carrister was the noblest heroine I've ever
    heard of in my day.

The Miraculous Escape of Robert Allan, the Fireman

'Twas in the year of 1888, and on October the
    fourteenth day,
That a fire broke out in a warehouse, and for hours
    blazed away;
And the warehouse, now destroyed, was occupied by the
    Messrs R. Wylie, Hill & Co.,
Situated in Buchanan Street, in the City of Glasgow.

The flames burst forth about three o'clock in the afternoon,
And intimation of the outbreak spread very soon;
And in the spectators' faces were depicted fear and
    consternation;
While the news flew like lightning to the Fire Brigade Station.

And when the Brigade reached the scene of the fire,
The merciless flames were ascending higher and higher,
Raging furiously in all the floors above the street,
And within twenty minutes the structure was destroyed by
    the burning heat.

Then the roof fell in, pushing out the front wall,
And the loud crash thereof frightened the spectators one
    and all,
Because it shook the neighbouring buildings to their
    foundation,
And caused throughout the City a great sensation.

And several men were injured by the falling of the wall,
And as the bystanders gazed thereon, it did their
    hearts appal;
But the poor fellows bore up bravely, without uttering
    a moan,
And with all possible speed they were conveyed home.

The firemen tried to play upon the building where the fire
    originated,
But, alas! their efforts were unfortunately frustrated,
Because they were working the hose pipes in a building
    occupied by Messrs Smith & Brown,
But the roof was fired, and amongst them it came
    crashing down.

And miraculously they escaped except one fireman,
The hero of the fire, named Robert Allan,
Who was carried with the debris down to the street floor,
And what he suffered must have been hard to endure.

He travelled to the fire in Buchanan Street,
On the first machine that was ordered, very fleet,

Along with Charles Smith and Dan. Ritchie,
And proceeded to Brown & Smith's buildings that were
    burning furiously.

And in the third floor of the building he took his stand
Most manfully, without fear, with the hose in his hand,
And played on the fire through a window in the gable
With all his might, the hero, as long as he was able.

And he remained there for about a quarter of an hour,
While from his hose upon the building the water did pour,
When, without the least warning, the floor gave way,
And down he went with it: oh, horror! and dismay!

And with the debris and flooring he got jammed,
But Charlie Smith and Dan. Ritchie quickly planned
To lower down a rope to him, without any doubt,
So, with a long pull and a strong pull, he was dragged out.

He thought he was jammed in for a very long time,
For, instead of being only two hours jammed, he thought
    'twas months nine,
But the brave hero kept up his spirits without any dread,
Then he was taken home in a cab, and put to bed.

Oh, kind Christians! think of Robert Allan, the heroic man,
For he certainly is a hero, deny it who can?
Because, although he was jammed, and in the midst of
    the flame,
He tells the world fearlessly he felt no pain.

The reason why, good people, he felt no pain
Is because he put his trust in God, to me it seems plain,
And in conclusion, I most earnestly pray,
That we will all put our trust in God, night and day.

And I hope that Robert Allan will do the same,
Because He saved him from being burnt while in the flame;
And all those that trust in God will do well,
And be sure to escape the pains of hell.

Adventures of King Robert the Bruce

King Robert the Bruce's deadly enemy, John of Lorn,
Joined the English with eight hundred Highlanders one
    fine morn,
All strong, hardy, and active fearless mountaineers,
But Bruce's men attacked them with swords and spears.

And while they were engaged, a new enemy burst
    upon them,
Like a torrent of raging water rushing down a rocky glen:
It was John of Lorn and his Highlanders that came
    upon them,
So the tide of battle was too much for them to stem.

And with savage yells they made the valley ring,
Then made a long circuit, and stole in behind the King.
Whirling their broadswords and Lochaber axes left and right;
And the enemy being thrice their number, they relinquished
    the fight.

Then to a certain house Bruce quickly hied,
And sitting by the door the housewife he spied;
And she asked him who he was, and he said, A wanderer,
Then she said, All wanderers are welcome here, kind sir.

Then the King said, Good dame, tell me the reason why,
How you respect all wanderers that chance to pass by,
And for whose sake you bear such favour to homeless men?
Then she said, King Robert the Bruce, if you want to ken,

The lawful King of this country, whom I hope to see;
Then Bruce said, My good woman, your King stands
    before thee;
And she said, Ah! sire, where are your men gone?
Then the King told her that he's come alone.

Then she said, Ah, my lawful King, this must not be,
For I have two stout sons, and they shall follow thee,
And fight to the death for your Majesty,
Aye, in faith, my good King, by land or sea.

Then she brought her sons before the King, and thus did say,
Now swear, my sons, to be true to your King without
    dismay;
Then they knelt and cried, Mother, we'll do as you desire,
We willingly will fight on behalf of our noble sire.

Who has been hunted like a felon by night and by day,
By foul plotters devising to take his life away;
But God will protect him in the midst of the strife,
And, mother dear, we'll fight for him during life.

Then the King said, Noble lads, it's you shall follow me,
And ye shall be near me by land or sea,
And for your loyalty towards me your mother I'll reward;
When all on a sudden the tramping of horses was heard.

Then the King heard voices he knew full well,
But what had fetched his friends there he couldn't tell;
'Twas Edward his brother and Lord Douglas, with one
    hundred and fifty men,
That had travelled far, to find their King, o'er mountain
    and glen.

And when they met they conversed on the events of the day,
Then the King unto them quickly did say,
If we knew where the enemy were, we would work them
    skaith;
    Then Lord James said, I'll lead you where they are, by
    my faith.

Then they marched upon the enemy just as the
    morning broke,
To a farm-house where they were lodged, and, with one
    bold stroke,
They, the Scots, rushed in and killed two-thirds of
    them dead;
And such was the life, alas! King Robert the Bruce led!

The Late
Sir John Ogilvy

Alas! Sir John Ogilvy is dead, aged eighty-seven,
But I hope his soul is now in heaven;
For he was a generous-hearted gentleman I am sure,
And, in particular, very kind unto the poor.

He was a Christian gentleman in every degree,
And, for many years, was an M.P. for Bonnie Dundee,
And, while he was an M.P., he didn't neglect
To advocate the rights of Dundee in every respect.

He was a public benefactor in many ways,
Especially in erecting an asylum for imbecile children to
   spend their days;
Then he handed the institution over as free,—
As a free gift and a boon to the people of Dundee.

He was chairman of several of the public boards in Dundee,
And among these were the Asylum Board and the Royal
   Infirmary;
In every respect he was a God-fearing true gentleman,
And to gainsay it there's nobody can.

He lived as a Christian gentleman in his time,
And he now lies buried in the family vault in Strathmartine;
But I hope his soul has gone aloft where all troubles cease,
Amongst the blessed saints where all is joy and peace.

To the people around Baldovan he will be a great loss,
Because he was a kind-hearted man and a Soldier of
   the Cross.
He had always a kind word for every one he met,
And the loss of such a good man will be felt with deep
   regret.

Because such men as Sir John Ogilvy are hard to be found,
Especially in Christian charity his large heart did abound,
Therefore a monument should be erected for him most
    handsome to behold,
And his good deeds engraven thereon in letters of gold.

The Pennsylvania Disaster

'Twas in the year of 1889, and in the month of June,
Ten thousand people met with a fearful doom,
By the bursting of a dam in Pennsylvania State,
And were burned, and drowned by the flood — oh! pity
    their fate!

The embankment of the dam was considered rather weak,
And by the swelled body of water the embankment did
    break,
And burst o'er the vally like a leaping river,
Which caused the spectators with fear to shiver.

And on rushed the mighty flood, like a roaring big wave,
Whilst the drowning people tried hard their lives to save;
But eight thousand were drowned, and their houses swept
    away,
While the spectators looked on, stricken with dismay.

And when the torrent dashed against the houses they
    instantly toppled o'er,
Then many of the houses caught fire, which made a
    terrific roar;
And two thousand people, by the fire, lost their lives,
Consisting of darling girls and boys, also men and
    their wives.

And when the merciless flood reached Johnstown it was
    fifty feet high,
While, in pitiful accents, the drowning people for help did cry;
But hundreds of corpses, by the flood, were swept away,
And Johnstown was blotted out like a child's toy house
    of clay.

Alas! There were many pitiful scenes enacted,
And many parents, for the loss of their children, have gone
    distracted,
Especially those that were burned in the merciless flame,
Their dear little ones they will never see again.

And among the sad scenes to be witnessed there,
Was a man and his wife in great despair,
Who had drawn from the burning mass a cradle of
    their child,
But, oh, heaven! their little one was gone, which almost
    drove them wild.

Oh, heaven! it was a pitiful and a most agonising sight,
To see parents struggling hard with all their might,
To save their little ones from being drowned,
But 'twas vain, the mighty flood engulfed them, with a
    roaring sound.

There was also a beautiful girl, the belle of Johnstown,
Standing in bare feet, on the river bank, sad and forlorn,
And clad in a loose petticoat, with a shawl over her head,
Which was all that was left her, because her parents
    were dead.

Her parents were drowned, and their property swept away
    with the flood,
And she was watching for them on the bank where she
    stood,
To see if they would rise to the surface of the water again,
But the dear girl's watching was all in vain.

And as for Conemaugh river, there's nothing could it surpass;
It was dammed up by a wall of corpses in a confused mass;

And the charred bodies could be seen dotting the
    burning debris,
While the flames and sparks ascended with a terrific hiss.

The pillaging of the houses in Johnstown is fearful to
    describe,
By the Hungarians and ghouls, and woe betide
Any person or party that interfered with them,
Because they were mad with drink, and yelling like tigers
    in a den.

And many were to be seen engaged in a hand-to-hand fight,
And drinking whisky, and singing wild songs, oh! what a
    shameful sight!
But a number of the thieves were lynched and shot
For robbing the dead of their valuables, which will not
    be forgot.

Mrs Ogle, like a heroine, in the telegraph office stood at
    her post,
And wired words of warning, else more lives would have
    been lost;
Besides she was warned to flee, but from her work she
    wouldn't stir,
Until at last the merciless flood engulfed her.

And as for the robbery and outrage at the hands of the
    ghouls,
I must mention Clara Barton and her band of merciful souls,
Who made their way fearlessly to the wounded in every
    street,
And the wounded and half-crazed survivors they kindly
    did treat.

Oh, heaven! it was a horrible sight, which will not be forgot,
So many people drowned and burned — oh! hard has been
    their lot!
But heaven's will must be done, I'll venture to say,
And accidents will happen until doomsday!

Attempted Assassination of the Queen

God prosper long our noble Queen,
And long may she reign!
Maclean he tried to shoot her,
But it was all in vain.

For God He turned the ball aside
Maclean aimed at her head;
And he felt very angry
Because he didn't shoot her dead.

There's a divinity that hedgeth a king.
And so it does seem.
And my opinion is, it has hedged
Our most gracious Queen.

Maclean must be a madman,
Which is obvious to be seen,
Or else he wouldn't have tried to shoot
Our most beloved Queen.

Victoria is a good Queen,
Which all her subjects know,
And for that God has protected her
From all her deadly foes.

She is noble and generous
Her subjects must confess;
There hasn't been her equal
Since the days of good Queen Bess.

Long may she be spared to roam
Among the bonnie Highland floral,
And spend many a happy day
In the palace of Balmoral.

Because she is very kind
To the old women there,
And allows them bread, tea, and sugar,
And each one to get a share.

And when they know of her coming,
Their hearts feel overjoy'd,
Because, in general, she finds work
For men that's unemploy'd.

And she also gives the gipsies money
While at Balmoral, I've been told,
And, mind ye, seldom silver,
But very often gold.

I hope God will protect her
By night and by day,
At home and abroad
When she's far away.

May He be as a hedge around her,
As He's been all along,
And let her live and die in peace
Is the end of my song.

The Royal Review

August 25, 1881

All hail to the Empress of India, Great Britain's Queen—
Long may she live in health, happy and serene—
That came from London, far away,
To review the Scottish Volunteers in grand array:
Most magnificent to be seen,
Near by Salisbury Crags and its pastures green,
Which will long be remembered by our gracious Queen—

And by the Volunteers, that came from far away,
Because it rain'd most of the day.
And with the rain their clothes were wet all through,
On the 25th day of August, at the Royal Review.
And to the Volunteers it was no lark,
Because they were ankle deep in mud in the Queen's Park,
Which proved to the Queen they were loyal true,
To endure such hardships at the Royal Review.

Oh! it was a most beautiful scene
To see the Forfarshire Artillery marching past the Queen;
Her Majesty with their steady marching felt content,
Especially when their arms to her they did present.

And the Inverness Highland Volunteers seemed verygran',
And marched by steady to a man
Amongst the mud without dismay,
And the rain pouring down on them all the way.
And the bands they did play, God Save the Queen,
Near by Holyrood Palace and the Queen's Park so green.

Success to our noble Scottish Volunteers!
I hope they will be spared for many long years,
And to Her Majesty always prove loyal and true,
As they have done for the second time at the Royal Review.

To take them in general, they behaved very well,
The more that the rain fell on them pell-mell.
They marched by Her Majesty in very grand array,
Which will be remembered for many a long day,
Bidding defiance to wind and rain,
Which adds the more fame to their name.

And I hope none of them will have cause to rue
The day that they went to the Royal Review.
And I'm sure Her Majesty ought to feel proud,
And in her praise she cannot speak too loud,
Because the more that it did rain they did not mourn,
Which caused Her Majesty's heart with joy to burn,
Because she knew they were loyal and true
For enduring such hardships at the Royal Review.

To Mr James Scrymgeour, Dundee

Success to James Scrymgeour,
He's a very good man,
And to gainsay it,
There's few people can;

Because he makes the hearts
Of the poor o'erjoyed
By trying to find work for them
When they're unemployed.

And to their complaints
He has always an attentive ear,
And ever ready to help them
When unto him they draw near.

And no matter what your occupation is,
Or what is your creed,
He will try to help you
In the time of need;

Because he has the fear
Of God within his heart,
And the man that fears God
Always takes the poor's part.

And blessed is the man
That is kind to the poor;
For his reward in heaven,
'Tis said in the Scripture, is sure.

And I hope heaven will be
Mr James Scrymgeour's reward;
For his struggles on behalf of the poor
Are really vexatious and hard.

For he is to be seen daily
Walking along our streets,
With a Christian-looking countenance,
And a kind word to all he meets.

Besides, he is void of all pride,
And wouldn't feel ashamed
To be seen with a beggar
Or a tinker walking by his side.

Fellow-citizens of Dundee,
Isn't it really very nice
To think of James Scrymgeour trying
To rescue fallen creatures from the paths of vice?

And in the winter he tries to provide
Hot dinners for the poor children of Dundee,
Who are starving with hunger no doubt,
And in the most abject poverty.

He is a little deaf, no doubt,
But not deaf to the cries of hungry men;
No! he always tries to do his best
To procure bread for them.

And at the Sabbath-morning free-breakfasts
He is often seen there,
Administering to the wants of the hungry,
And joining in prayer.

He is a man of noble principles,
As far as I can think,
And the noblest principle he has got
Is, he abhors the demon drink.

And, in my opinion, he is right
As far as I can see,
And I hereby proclaim that such a man
Is an honour to Dundee:

Because he is always working
For the poor people's good,
Kind soul, trying hard
To procure for them clothing and food.

Success to him and his family,
And may God them defend:
Why? fellow-citizens of Dundee,
Because he is the poor man's friend.

The Collision in the English Channel

'Twas on a Sunday morning, and in the year of 1888,
The steamer "Saxmundham," laden with coal and coke
    for freight,
Was run into amidships by the Norwegian barque "Nor,"
And sunk in the English Channel, while the storm fiend
    did roar.

She left Newcastle on Friday, in November, about
    two o'clock,
And proceeded well on her way until she received a shock;
And the effects of the collision were so serious within,
That, within twenty minutes afterwards, with water she was
    full to the brim.

The effects of the collision were so serious the water couldn't
    be staunched,
So immediately the "Saxmundham's" jolly-boat was launched;
While the brave crew were busy, and loudly did clatter,
Because, at this time, the stem of the steamer was
    under water.

Then the bold crew launched the lifeboat, without dismay,
While their hearts did throb, but not a word did they say;
They tried to launch the port lifeboat, but in that they failed,
Owing to the heavy sea, so their sad fate they bewailed.

Then into the jolly-boat and lifeboat jumped fifteen men
    in all,
And immediately the steamer foundered, which did their
    hearts appal,
As the good ship sank beneath the briny wave,
But they thanked God fervently that did them save.

Oh! it was a miracle how any of them were saved,
but it was by the aid of God, and how the crew behaved;
Because God helps those that help themselves,
And those that don't try to do so are silly elves.

So the two boats cruised about for some time,
Before it was decided to pull for St. Catherine;
And while cruising about they must have been ill,
But they succeeded in picking up an engineer and fireman,
    also Captain Milne.

And at daybreak on Sunday morning the men in the lifeboat
Were picked up by the schooner "Waterbird" as towards
    her they did float,
And landed at Weymouth, and made all right
By the authorities, who felt for them in their sad plight.

But regarding the barque "Nor," to her I must return,
And, no doubt, for the drowned men, many will mourn;
Because the crew's sufferings must have been great,
Which, certainly, is soul-harrowing to relate.

The ill-fated barque was abandoned in a sinking state,
But all her crew were saved, which I'm happy to relate;
They were rescued by the steamer "Hagbrook" in the
    afternoon,
When after taking to their boats, and brought to Portland
    very soon.

The barque "Nor" was bound from New York to Stettin,
And when she struck the "Saxmundham," oh! what
    terrible din!
Because the merciless water did rush in,
Then the ship carpenters to patch the breach did begin.

But alas! all their efforts proved in vain,
For still the water did on them gain;
Still they resolved to save her whatever did betide,
But, alas! the ill-fated "Nor" sank beneath the tide.

But thanks be to God, the major part of the men have
    been saved,
And all honour to both crews that so manfully behaved;
And may God protect the mariner by night and by day
When on the briny deep, far, far away!

The Execution of James Graham, Marquis of Montrose

A Historical Poem

'Twas in the Year of 1650, and on the twenty-first of May,
The city of Edinburgh was put into a state of dismay
By the noise of drums and trumpets, which on the air arose,
That the great sound attracted the notice of Montrose.

Who enquired at the Captain of the guard the cause of it,
Then the officer told him as he thought most fit,
That the Parliament dreading an attempt might be made to
    rescue him,
The soldiers were called out to arms, and that had made
    the din.

Do I, said Montrose, continue such a terror still?
Now when these good men are about my blood to spill,
But let them look to themselves, for after I am dead,
Their wicked consciences will be in continual dread.

After partaking of a hearty breakfast, he commenced
    his toilet,
Which, in his greatest trouble, he seldom did forget.
And while in the act of combing his hair,
He was visited by the Clerk Register, who made him stare,
When he told him he shouldn't be so particular with his head,
For in a few hours he would be dead;
But Montrose replied, While my head is my own I'll dress it
    at my ease,
And tomorrow, when it becomes yours, treat it as you
    please.

He was waited upon by the Magistrates of the city,
But, alas! for him they had no pity.
He was habited in a superb cloak, ornamented with gold and
    silver lace;
And before the hour of execution an immense assemblage of
    people were round the place.

From the prison, bareheaded, in a cart, they conveyed him
    along the Watergate
To the place of execution on the High Street, where about
    thirty thousand people did wait,
Some crying and sighing, a most pitiful sight to see,
All waiting patiently to see the executioner hang Montrose,
    a man of high degree.

Around the place of execution, all of them were deeply
    affected,
But Montrose, the noble hero, seemed not the least dejected;
And when on the scaffold he had, says his biographer
    Wishart,
Such a grand air and majesty, which made the people start.

As the fatal hour was approaching when he had to bid the
    world adieu,

He told the executioner to make haste and get quickly
    through,
But the executioner smiled grimly, but spoke not a word,
Then he tied the Book of Montrose's Wars round his neck
    with a cord.

Then he told the executioner his foes would remember
    him hereafter,
And he was as well pleased as if his Majesty had made him
    Knight of the Garter;
Then he asked to be allowed to cover his head,
But he was denied permission, yet he felt no dread.

He then asked leave to keep on his cloak,
But was also denied, which was a most grievous stroke;
Then he told the Magistrates, if they could invent any more
    tortures for him,
He would endure them all for the cause he suffered, and
    think it no sin.

On arriving at the top of the ladder with great firmness,
His heroic appearance greatly did the bystanders impress,
Then Montrose asked the executioner how long his body
    would be suspended,
Three hours was the answer, but Montrose was not the least
    offended.

Then he presented the executioner with three or four pieces
    of gold,
Whom he freely forgave, to his honour be it told,
And told him to throw him off as soon as he uplifted
    his hands,
While the executioner watched the fatal signal, and in
    amazement stands.

And on the noble patriot raising his hands, the executioner
    began to cry,
Then quickly he pulled the rope down from the gibbet
    on high,
And around Montrose's neck he fixed the rope very gently,
And in an instant the great Montrose was launched
    into eternity.

Then the spectators expressed their disapprobation by
    general groan,
And they all dispersed quietly, and wended their way home
And his bitterest enemies that saw his death that day,
Their hearts were filled with sorrow and dismay.

Thus died, at the age of thirty-eight, James Graham,
    Marquis of Montrose,
Who was brought to a premature grave by his bitter foes;
A commander who had acquired great military glory
In a short space of time, which cannot be equalled in story.

The
Beautiful
Sun

Beautiful Sun! with thy golden rays,
To God, the wise creator, be all praise;
For thou nourisheth all the creation,
Wherever there is found to be animation.

Without thy heat we could not live,
Then praise to God we ought to give;
For thou makest the fruits and provisions to grow,
To nourish all creatures on earth below.

Thou makest the hearts of the old feel glad,
Likewise the young child and the lad,
And the face of Nature to look green and gay,
And the little children to sport and play.

Thou also giveth light unto the Moon,
Which certainly is a very great boon

To all God's creatures here below,
Throughout the world where'er they go.

How beautiful thou look'st on a summer morn,
When thou sheddest thy effulgence among the yellow corn,
Also upon lake, and river, and the mountain tops,
Whilst thou leavest behind the most lovely dewdrops!

How beautiful thou seem'st in the firmament above,
As I gaze upon thee, my heart fills with love
To God, the great Creator, Who has placed thee there,
Who watches all His creatures with an eye of care!

Thou makest the birds to sing on the tree,
Also by meadow, mountain, and lea;
And the lark high poised up in air,
Carolling its little song with its heart free from care.

Thou makest the heart of the shepherd feel gay
As he watches the little lambkins at their innocent play;
While he tends them on the hillside all day,
Taking care that none of them shall go astray.

Thou cheerest the weary traveller while on his way
During the livelong summer day,
As he admires the beautiful scenery while passing along
And singing to himself a stave of a song.

Thou cheerest the tourist while amongst the Highland hills,
As he views their beautiful sparkling rills
Glittering like diamonds by thy golden rays,
While the hills seem to offer up to God their praise.

While the bee from flower to flower does roam
To gather honey, and carry it home;
While it hums its little song in the beautiful sunshine,
And seemingly to thank the Creator divine —

For the honey it hath gathered during the day,
In the merry month of May,
When the flowers are in full bloom,
Also the sweet honeysuckle and the broom.

How beautiful thy appearance while setting in the west,
Whilst encircled with red and azure, 'tis then thou
    look'st best!
Then let us all thank God for thy golden light
In our prayers every morning and night!

The Clepington Catastrophe

'Twas on a Monday morning, and in the year of 1884,
That a fire broke out in Bailie Bradford's store,
Which contained bales of jute and large quantities of waste,
Which the brave firemen ran to extinguish in great haste.

They left their wives that morning without any dread,
Never thinking, at the burning pile, they would be killed dead
By the falling of the rickety and insecure walls;
When I think of it, kind Christians, my heart it appals!

Because it has caused widows and their families to shed
    briny tears,
For there hasn't been such a destructive fire for many years;
Whereby four brave firemen have perished in the fire,
And for better fathers or husbands no family could desire.

'Twas about five o'clock in the morning the fire did break out,
While one of the workmen was inspecting the premises round
    about—
Luckily before any one had begun their work for the day—
So he instantly gave the alarm without delay.

At that time only a few persons were gathered on the spot,
But in a few minutes some hundreds were got,
Who came flying in all directions, and in great dismay;
So they help'd to put out the fire without delay.

But the spreading flames, within the second flats, soon began
    to appear,
Which filled the spectators' hearts with sympathy and fear,
Lest any one should lose their life in the merciless fire,
When they saw it bursting out and ascending higher and
    higher.

Captain Ramsay, of the Dundee Fire Brigade, was the first
    to arrive,
And under his directions the men seemed all alive,
For they did their work heroically, with all their might
    and main,
In the midst of blinding smoke and the burning flame.

As soon as the catastrophe came to be known,
The words, Fire! Fire! from every mouth were blown;
And a cry of despair rang out on the morning air,
When they saw the burning pile with its red fiery glare.

While a dense cloud of smoke seemed to darken the sky,
And the red glaring flame ascended up on high,
Which made the scene appear weird-like around;
While from the spectators was heard a murmuring sound.

But the brave firemen did their duty manfully to the last,
And plied the water on the burning pile, copiously and fast;
But in a moment, without warning, the front wall gave way,
Which filled the people's hearts with horror and dismay:

Because four brave firemen were killed instantaneously
    on the spot,
Which by the spectators will never be forgot;
While the Fire Fiend laughingly did hiss and roar,
As he viewed their mangled bodies, with the *debris*
    covered o'er.

But in the midst of dust and fire they did their duty well,
Aye! in the midst of a shower of bricks falling on them
  pell-mell,
Until they were compelled to let the water-hose go;
While the blood from their bruised heads and arms did flow.

But brave James Fyffe held on to the hose until the last,
And when found in the *debris,* the people stood aghast.
When they saw him lying dead, with the hose in his hand,
Their tears for him they couldn't check nor yet command.

Oh, heaven! I must confess it was no joke
To see them struggling in the midst of suffocating smoke,
Each man struggling hard, no doubt, to save his life,
When he thought of his dear children and his wife.

But still the merciless flame shot up higher and higher;
Oh, God! it is terrible and cruel to perish by fire;
Alas! it was saddening and fearful to behold,
When I think of it, kind Christians, it makes my blood
  run cold.

What makes the death of Fyffe the more distressing,
He was going to be the groomsman at his sister's bridal
  dressing,
Who was going to be married the next day;
But, alas! the brave hero's life was taken away.

But accidents will happen by land and by sea.
Therefore, to save ourselves from accidents, we needn't try
  to flee,
For whatsoever God has ordained will come to pass;
For instance, ye may be killed by a stone or a piece of glass.

I hope the Lord will provide for the widows in their distress,
For they are to be pitied, I really must confess;
And I hope the public of Dundee will lend them a helping
  hand;
To help the widows and the fatherless is God's command.

The Battle
Of Bannockburn

Sir Robert the Bruce at Bannockburn
Beat the English in every wheel and turn,
And made them fly in great dismay
From off the field without delay.

The English were a hundred thousand strong,
And King Edward passed through the Lowlands all along,
Determined to conquer Scotland, it was his desire,
And then to restore it to his own empire.

King Edward brought numerous waggons in his train,
Expecting that most of the Scottish army would be slain,
Hoping to make the rest prisoners, and carry them away
In waggon-loads to London without delay.

The Scottish army did not amount to more than thirty
    thousand strong;
But Bruce had confidence he'd conquer his foes ere long;
So, to protect his little army, he thought it was right
To have deep-dug pits made in the night;

And caused them to be overlaid with turf and brushwood
Expecting the plan would prove effectual where his little
    army stood,
Waiting patiently for the break of day,
All willing to join in the deadly fray.

Bruce stationed himself at the head of the reserve,
Determined to conquer, but never to swerve,
And by his side were brave Kirkpatrick and true
    De Longueville,
Both trusty warriors, firm and bold, who would never him beguile.

By daybreak the whole of the English army came in view,
Consisting of archers and horsemen, bold and true;
The main body was led on by King Edward himself,
An avaricious man, and fond of pelf.

The Abbot of Inchaffray celebrated mass,
And all along the Scottish lines barefoot he did pass,
With the crucifix in his hand, a most beautiful sight to see,
Exhorting them to trust in God, and He would set them free.

Then the Scottish army knelt down on the field,
And King Edward he thought they were going to yield,
And he felt o'erjoyed, and cried to Earl Percy,
"See! See! the Scots are crying for mercy."

But Percy said, "Your Majesty need not make such a fuss,
They are crying for mercy from God, not from us;
For, depend upon it, they will fight to a man, and find
    their graves
Rather than yield to become your slaves."

Then King Edward ordered his horsemen to charge,
Thirty thousand in number, it was very large;
They thought to o'erwhelm them ere they could rise from
    their knees,
But they met a different destiny, which did them displease;
For the horsemen fell into the spik'd pits in the way,
And, with broken ranks and confusion, they all fled away.

But few of them escap'd death from the spik'd pits,
For the Scots with their swords hack'd them to bits;
De Valence was overthrown and carried off the field,
Then King Edward he thought it was time to yield.

And he uttered a fearful cry
To his gay archers near by,
Ho! archers! draw your arrows to the head,
And make sure to kill them dead;
Forward, without dread, and make them fly,
Saint George for England, be our cry!

Then the arrows from their bows swiftly did go,
And fell amongst them as thick as the flakes of snow;
Then Bruce he drew his trusty blade,
And in heroic language said,
Forward! my heroes, bold and true!

And break the archer's ranks through and through!
And charge them boldly with your swords in hand,
And chase these vultures from off our land,
And make King Edward mourn
The day he came to Bannockburn.

So proud Edward on his milk-white steed,
One of England's finest breed,
Coming here in grand array,
With horsemen bold and archers gay,
Thinking he will us dismay,
And sweep everything before him in his way;
But I swear by yon blessed sun
I'll make him and his army run
From off the field of Bannockburn.

By St. Andrew and our God most high,
We'll conquer these epicures or die!
And make them fly like chaff before the wind
Until they can no refuge find;
And beat them off the field without delay,
Like lions bold and heroes gay.
Upon them!—charge!—follow me,
For Scotland's rights and liberty!

Then the Scots charged them with sword in hand,
And made them fly from off their land;
And King Edward was amazed at the sight,
And he got wounded in the fight;
And he cried, Oh, heaven! England's lost, and I'm undone,
Alas! alas! where shall I run?
Then he turned his horse, and rode on afar,
And never halted till he reached Dunbar.

Then Bruce he shouted, Victory!
We have gained our rights and liberty;
And thanks be to God above
That we have conquered King Edward this day,
A usurper that does not us love.

Then the Scots did shout and sing,
Long live Sir Robert Bruce our King!
That made King Edward mourn
The day he came to Bannockburn!

The
Christmas
Goose

Mr Smiggs was a gentleman,
And he lived in London town;
His wife she was a good kind soul,
And seldom known to frown.

'Twas on Christmas eve,
And Smiggs and his wife lay cosy in bed,
When the thought of buying a goose
Came into his head.

So the next morning,
Just as the sun rose,
He jump'd out of bed,
And he donn'd his clothes,

Saying, "Peggy, my dear,
You need not frown,
For I'll buy you the best goose
In all London Town."

So away to the poultry shop he goes,
And bought the goose, as he did propose,
And for it he paid one crown,
The finest, he thought, in London town.

When Smiggs bought the goose
He suspected no harm,
But a naughty boy stole it
From under his arm.

Then Smiggs he cried, "Stop, thief!
Come back with my goose!"
But the naughty boy laugh'd at him,
And gave him much abuse.

But a policeman captur'd the naughty boy,
And gave the goose to Smiggs,
And said he was greatly bother'd
By a set of juvenile prigs.

So the naughty boy was put in prison
For stealing the goose,
And got ten days' confinement
Before he got loose.

So Smiggs ran home to his dear Peggy,
Saying, "Hurry, and get this fat goose ready,
That I have bought for one crown;
So, my darling, you need not frown."

"Dear Mr Smiggs, I will not frown:
I'm sure 'tis cheap for one crown,
Especially at Christmas time—
Oh! Mr Smiggs, it's really fine."

"Peggy, it is Christmas time,
So let us drive dull care away,
For we have got a Christmas goose,
So cook it well, I pray.

"No matter how the poor are clothed,
Or if they starve at home,
We'll drink our wine, and eat our goose,
Aye, and pick it to the bone."

The Battle
Of Culloden:

A Historical Poem

'Twas in the year of 1746, and in April the 14th day,
That Prince Charles Stuart and his army marched on
   without delay
And on the 14th of April they encamped on Culloden Moor,
But the army felt hungry, and no food could they procure.

And the calls of hunger could not brook delay,
So they resolved to have food, come what may;
They, poor men, were hungry and in sore distress,
And many of them, as well as officers, slipped off to
   Inverness.

The Prince gave orders to bring provisions to the field,
Because he knew without food his men would soon yield
To the pangs of hunger, besides make them feel discontent,
So some of them began to search the neighbourhood for
   refreshment.

And others, from exhaustion, lay down on the ground,
And soon in the arms of Morpheus they were sleeping sound;
While the Prince and some of his officers began to search
   for food,
And got some bread and whisky, which they thought
   very good.

The Highland army was drawn up in three lines in
   grand array,
All eager for the fray in April the 16th day,
Consisting of the Athole Brigade, who made a grand display
On the field of Culloden on that ever-memorable day.
Likewise the Camerons, Stewarts, and Macintoshes,
   Maclachlans and Macleans,
And John Roy Stewart's regiment, united into one, these are
   their names;

Besides the Macleods, Chisholms, Macdonalds of Clanranald
   and Glengarry,
Also the noble chieftain Keppoch, all eager the English
   to harry.

The second line of the Highland army formed in column on
   the right,
Consisting of the Gordons, under Lord Lewis Gordon, ready
   for the fight;
Besides the French Royal Scots, the Irish Piquets or Brigade,
Also Lord Kilmarnock's Foot Guards, and a grand show
   they made.

Lord John Drummond's regiment and Glenbucket's were
   flanked on the right
By Fitz-James's Dragoons and Lord Elcho's Horse Guards, a
   magnificent sight;
And on the left by the Perth squadron under Lord
   Strathallan,
A fine body of men, and resolved to fight to a man.

And there was Pitsligo, and the Prince's body guards under
   Lord Balmerino,
And the third line was commanded by General Stapleton, a
   noble hero;
Besides, Lord Ogilvie was in command of the third line
   or reserve,
Consisting of the Duke of Perth's regiment and Lord
   Ogilvy's—men of firm nerve.

The Prince took his station on a very small eminence.
Surrounded by a troop of Fitz-James's horse for his defense,
Where he had a complete view of the whole field of battle,
Where he could see the front line and hear the cannons
   rattle.

Both armies were about the distance of a mile from
   each other,
All ready to commence the fight, brother against brother,
Each expecting that the other would advance
To break a sword in combat, or shiver a lance.

To encourage his men the Duke of Cumberland rode along
   the line,
Addressing himself hurriedly to every regiment, which was
   really sublime;
Telling his men to use their bayonets, and allow the
   Highlanders to mingle with them,
And look terror to the rebel foe, and have courage, my men.

Then Colonel Belford of the Duke's army opened fire from
   the front line,
After the Highlanders had been firing for a short time;
The Duke ordered Colonel Belford to continue the
   cannonade,
To induce the Highlanders to advance, because they seemed
   afraid.

And with a cannon-ball the Prince's horse was shot above
   the knee,
So that Charles had to change him for another immediately;
And one of his servants who led the horse was killed on
   the spot,
Which by Prince Charles Stuart was never forgot.

'Tis said in history, before the battle began
The Macdonalds claimed the right as their due of leading
   the van,
And because they wouldn't be allowed, with anger their
   hearts did burn,
Because Bruce conferred that honour upon the Macdonalds
   at the Battle of Bannockburn.

And galled beyond endurance by the fire of the English
   that day,
Which caused the Highlanders to cry aloud to be led forward
   without delay,
Until at last the brave Clan Macintosh rushed forward
   without dismay,
While with grape-shot from a side battery hundreds were
   swept away.

Then the Athole Highlanders and the Camerons rushed in
   sword in hand,

And broke through Barrel's and Monro's regiments, a sight
　　most grand;
After breaking through these two regiments they gave up
　　the contest,
Until at last they had to retreat after doing their best.

Then, stung to the quick, the brave Keppoch, who was
　　abandoned by his clan,
Boldly advanced with his drawn sword in hand, the
　　brave man.
But, alas! he was wounded by a musket-shot, which he
　　manfully bore,
And in the fight he received another shot, and fell to rise
　　no more.

Nothing could be more disastrous to the Prince that day,
Owing to the Macdonalds refusing to join in the deadly fray;
Because if they had all shown their wonted courage that day,
The proud Duke of Cumberland's army would have been
　　forced to run away.

And, owing to the misconduct of the Macdonalds, the
　　Highlanders had to yield,
And General O'Sullivan laid hold of Charles's horse, and led
　　him off the field,
As the whole army was now in full retreat,
And with the deepest concern the Prince lamented his
　　sore defeat.

Prince Charles Stuart, of fame and renown,
You might have worn Scotland's crown,
If the Macdonalds and Glengarry at Culloden had
　　proved true;
But, being too ambitious for honour, that they didn't do,
Which, I am sorry to say, proved most disastrous to you,
Looking to the trials and struggles you passed through.

———————————————————————

The Death of Lord and Lady Dalhousie

Alas! Lord and Lady Dalhousie are dead, and buried at last.
Which causes many people to feel a little downcast;
And both lie side by side in one grave,
But I hope God in His goodness their souls will save.

And may He protect their children that are left behind,
And may they always food and raiment find;
And from the paths of virtue may they ne'er be led,
And may they always find a house wherein to lay their head.

Lord Dalhousie was a man worthy of all praise,
And to his memory I hope a monument the people will raise,
That will stand for many ages to come
To commemorate the good deeds he has done.

He was beloved by men of high and low degree,
Especially in Forfarshire by his tenantry;
And by many of the inhabitants in and around Dundee,
Because he was affable in temper, and void of all vanity.

He had great affection for his children, also his wife,
'Tis said he loved her as dear as his life;
And I trust they are now in heaven above,
Where all is joy, peace, and love.

At the age of fourteen he resolved to go to sea,
So he entered the training ship Britannia belonging the navy,
And entered as a midshipman as he considered most fit
Then passed through the course of training with the
    greatest credit.

In a short time he obtained the rank of lieutenant,
Then to her Majesty's ship Galatea he was sent;

Which was under the command of the Duke of Edinburgh,
And during his service there he felt but little sorrow.

And from that he was promoted to be commander of
   the Britannia,
And was well liked by the men, for what he said was law;
And by him Prince Albert Victor and Prince George received
   a naval education,
Which met with the Prince of Wales' most hearty
   approbation.

'Twas in the year 1877 he married the Lady Ada
   Louisa Bennett,
And by marrying that noble lady he ne'er did regret;
And he was ever ready to give his service in any way,
Most willingly and cheerfully by night or by day.

'Twas in the year of 1887, and on Thursday the 1st
   of December,
Which his relatives and friends will long remember
That were present at the funeral in Cockpen churchyard,
Because they had for the noble Lord a great regard.

About eleven o'clock the remains reached Dalhousie,
And were met by a body of the tenantry;
They conveyed them inside the building, all seemingly
   woebegone,
And among those that sent wreaths was Lord
   Claude Hamilton.

Those that sent wreaths were but very few,
But one in particular was the Duke of Buccleuch;
Besides Dr. Herbert Spencer, and Countess Rosebery,
   and Lady Bennett,
Which no doubt were sent by them with heartfelt regret.

Besides those that sent wreaths in addition were the Earl and
   Countess of Aberdeen,
Especially the Prince of Wales' was most lovely to be seen,
And the Earl of Dalkeith's wreath was very pretty too,
With a mixture of green and white flowers, beautiful to view.

Amongst those present at the interment were
   Mr. Marjoribanks, M.P.
Also ex-Provost Ballingall from Bonnie Dundee;
Besides the Honourable W. G. Colville, representing the
   Duke and Duchess of Edinburgh,
While in every one's face standing at the grave was
   depicted sorrow.

The funeral service was conducted in the Church of Cockpen
By the Rev. J. Crabb, of St. Andrew's Episcopal Church,
   town of Brechin;
And as the two coffins were lowered into their last
   resting place,
Then the people retired with sad hearts at a quick pace.

A Tribute to Mr Murphy and the Blue Ribbon Army

All hail to Mr Murphy, he is a hero brave,
That has crossed the mighty Atlantic wave,
For what purpose let me pause and think—
I answer, to warn the people not to taste strong drink.

And, I'm sure, if they take his advice, they never will rue
The day they joined the Blue Ribbon Army in the year 1882;
And I hope to their colours they will always prove true.
And shout, Hurrah! for Mr Murphy and the Ribbon of Blue.

What is strong drink? Let me think—I answer 'tis a thing
From whence the majority of evils spring,
And causes many a fireside with boisterous talk to ring,
And leaves behind it a deadly sting.

Some people do say it is good when taken in moderation,
But, when taken to excess, it leads to tribulation,
Also to starvation and loss of reputation,
Likewise your eternal soul's damnation.

The drunkard, he says he can't give it up,
For I must confess temptation's in the cup;
But he wishes to God it was banished from the land,
While he holds the cup in his trembling hand.

And he exclaims in the agony of his soul—
Oh, God, I cannot myself control
From this most accurs'd cup!
Oh, help me, God, to give it up!

Strong drink to the body can do no good;
It defiles the blood, likewise the food,
And causes the drunkard with pain to groan,
Because it extracts the marrow from the bone:

And hastens him on to a premature grave,
Because to the cup he is bound a slave;
For the temptation is hard to thole,
And by it he will lose his immortal soul.

The more's the pity, I must say,
That so many men and women are by it led astray,
And decoyed from the paths of virtue and led on to vice
By drinking too much alcohol and acting unwise.

Good people all, of every degree,
I pray, ye all be warned by me:
I advise ye all to pause and think,
And never more to taste strong drink.

Because the drunkard shall never inherit the kingdom of God
And whosoever God loves he chastens with his rod:
Therefore, be warned, and think in time,
And don't drink any more whisky, rum, or wine.

But go at once—make no delay,
And join the Blue Ribbon Army without dismay,

And rally round Mr Murphy, and make a bold stand,
And help to drive the Bane of Society from our land.

I wish Mr Murphy every success,
Hoping he will make rapid progress;
And to the Blue Ribbon Army may he always prove true,
And adhere to his colours—the beautiful blue.

Glasgow

Beautiful city of Glasgow, with your streets so neat
  and clean,
Your stately mansions, and beautiful Green!
Likewise your beautiful bridges across the river Clyde,
And on your bonnie banks I would like to reside.

Chorus—

Then away to the West—to the beautiful West!
To the fair city of Glasgow that I like the best,
Where the river Clyde rolls on to the sea,
And the lark and the blackbird whistle with glee.

'Tis beautiful to see the ships passing to and fro,
Laden with goods for the high and low;
So let the beautiful city of Glasgow flourish,
And may the inhabitants always find food their bodies
  to nourish.

Chorus.

The statue of the Prince of Orange is very grand,
Looking terror to the foe, with a truncheon in his hand,
And well mounted on a noble steed, which stands in
  the Trongate,
And holding up its foreleg, I'm sure it looks first-rate.

Chorus.

Then there's the Duke of Wellington's statue in Royal
    Exchange Square—
It is a beautiful statue I without fear declare,
Besides inspiring and most magnificent to view,
Because he made the French fly at the battle of Waterloo.

Chorus.

And as for the statue of Sir Walter Scott that stands in
    George Square,
It is a handsome statue—few can with it compare,
And most elegant to be seen,
And close beside it stands the statue of Her Majesty
    the Queen.

Chorus.

Then there's the statue of Robert Burns in George Square,
And the treatment he received when living was very unfair;
Now, when he's dead, Scotland's sons for him do mourn,
But, alas! unto them he can never return.

Chorus.

Then as for Kelvin Grove, it is most lovely to be seen
With its beautiful flowers and trees so green,
And a magnificent water-fountain spouting up very high,
Where the people can quench their thirst when they feel dry.

Chorus.

Beautiful city of Glasgow, I now conclude my muse,
And to write in praise of thee my pen does not refuse;
And, without fear of contradiction, I will venture to say
You are the second grandest city in Scotland at the
    present day!

Chorus.

Grace Darling:
or the Wreck of the
"Forfarshire"

As the night was beginning to close in one rough September
day
In the year of 1838, a steamer passed through the Fairway
Between the Farne Islands and the coast, on her passage
   northwards;
But the wind was against her, and the steamer
   laboured hard.

There she laboured in the heavy sea against both wind
   and tide,
Whilst a dense fog enveloped her on every side;
And the mighty billows made her timbers creak,
Until at last, unfortunately, she sprung a leak.

Then all hands rushed to the pumps, and wrought with might
   and main.
But the water, alas! alarmingly on them did gain;
And the thick sleet was driving across the raging sea,
While the wind it burst upon them in all its fury.

And the fearful gale and the murky aspect of the sky
Caused the passengers on board to lament and sigh
As the sleet drove thick, furious, and fast,
And as the waves surged mountains high, they stood aghast.

And the screaming of the sea-birds foretold a
   gathering storm,
And the passengers, poor souls, looked pale and forlorn,
And on every countenance was depicted woe
As the "Forfarshire" steamer was pitched to and fro.

And the engine-fires with the water were washed out;
Then, as the tide set strongly in, it wheeled the vessel about,

And the ill-fated vessel drifted helplessly along;
But the fog cleared up a little as the night wore on.

Then the terror-stricken crew saw the breakers ahead,
And all thought of being saved from them fled;
And the Farne lights were shining hazily through the gloom,
While in the fore-cabin a woman lay with two children in
    a swoon.

Before the morning broke, the "Forfarshire" struck upon
    a rock,
And was dashed to pieces by a tempestuous shock,
Which raised her for a moment, and dashed her down again,
Then the ill-starred vessel was swallowed up in the
    briny main.

Before the vessel broke up, some nine or ten of the
    crew intent
To save their lives, or perish in the attempt,
Lowered one of the boats while exhausted and forlorn,
And, poor souls, were soon lost sight of in the storm.

Around the windlass on the forecastle some dozen poor
    wretches clung,
And with despair and grief their weakly hearts were rung
As the merciless sea broke o'er them every moment;
But God in His mercy to them Grace Darling sent.

By the first streak of dawn she early up had been,
And happened to look out upon the stormy scene,
And she descried the wreck through the morning gloom;
But she resolved to rescue them from such a perilous doom.

Then she cried, Oh! father dear, come here and see
    the wreck,
See, here take the telescope, and you can inspect;
Oh! father, try and save them, and heaven will you bless;
But, my darling, no help can reach them in such a storm
    as this.

Oh! my kind father, you will surely try and save
These poor souls from a cold and watery grave;

Oh! I cannot sit to see them perish before mine eyes,
And, for the love of heaven, do not my pleading despise!

Then old Darling yielded, and launched the little boat,
And high on the big waves the boat did float;
Then Grace and her father took each an oar in hand,
And to see Grace Darling rowing the picture was grand.

And as the little boat to the sufferers drew near,
Poor souls, they tried to raise a cheer;
But as they gazed upon the heroic Grace,
The big tears trickled down each sufferer's face.

And nine persons were rescued almost dead with the cold
By modest and lovely Grace Darling, that heroine bold;
The survivors were taken to the light-house, and remained
    there two days,
And every one of them was loud in Grace Darling's praise.

Grace Darling was a comely lass, with long, fair floating hair,
With soft blue eyes, and shy, and modest rare;
And her countenance was full of sense and genuine
    kindliness,
With a noble heart, and ready to help suffering creatures
    in distress.

But, alas! three years after her famous exploit,
Which, to the end of time, will never be forgot,
Consumption, that fell destroyer, carried her away
To heaven, I hope, to be an angel for every and aye.

Before she died, scores of suitors in marriage sought
    her hand;
But no, she'd rather live in Longstone light-house on
    Farne island,
And there she lived and died with her father and mother,
And for her equal in true heroism we cannot find another.

The Railway Bridge of the Silvery Tay

Beautiful Railway Bridge of the Silvery Tay!
With your numerous arches and pillars in so grand array,
And your central girders, which seem to the eye
To be almost towering to the sky.
The greatest wonder of the day,
And a great beautification to the River Tay,
Most beautiful to be seen,
Near by Dundee and the Magdalen Green.

Beautiful Railway Bridge of the Silvery Tay!
That has caused the Emperor of Brazil to leave
His home far away, *incognito* in his dress,
And view thee ere he passed along *en route* to Inverness.

Beautiful Railway Bridge of the Silvery Tay!
The longest of the present day
That has ever crossed o'er a tidal river stream,
Most gigantic to be seen,
Near by Dundee and the Magdalen Green.

Beautiful Railway Bridge of the Silvery Tay!
Which will cause great rejoicing on the opening day,
And hundreds of people will come from far away,
Also the Queen, most gorgeous to be seen,
Near by Dundee and the Magdalen Green.

Beautiful Railway Bridge of the Silvery Tay!
And prosperity to Provost Cox, who has given
Thirty thousand pounds and upwards away
In helping to erect the Bridge of the Tay,
Most handsome to be seen,
Near by Dundee and the Magdalen Green.

Beautiful Railway Bridge of the Silvery Tay!
I hope that God will protect all passengers

By night and by day,
And that no accident will befall them while crossing
The Bridge of the Silvery Tay,
For that would be most awful to be seen
Near by Dundee and the Magdalen Green.

Beautiful Railway Bridge of the Silvery Tay!
And prosperity to Messrs Bouche and Grothe,
The famous engineers of the present day,
Who have succeeded in erecting the Railway
Bridge of the Silvery Tay,
Which stands unequalled to be seen
Near by Dundee and the Magdalen Green.

The Tay
Bridge Disaster

Beautiful Railway Bridge of the Silv'ry Tay!
Alas! I am very sorry to say
That ninety lives have been taken away
On the last Sabbath day of 1879,
Which will be remember'd for a very long time.

'Twas about seven o'clock at night,
And the wind it blew with all its might,
And the rain came pouring down,
And the dark clouds seem'd to frown,
And the Demon of the air seem'd to say—
"I'll blow down the Bridge of Tay."

When the train left Edinburgh
The passengers' hearts were light and felt no sorrow,
But Boreas blew a terrific gale,
Which made their hearts for to quail,
And many of the passengers with fear did say—
"I hope God will send us safe across the Bridge of Tay."

But when the train came near to Wormit Bay,
Boreas he did loud and angry bray,
And shook the central girders of the Bridge of Tay
On the last Sabbath day of 1879,
Which will be remember'd for a very long time.

So the train sped on with all its might,
And Bonnie Dundee soon hove in sight,
And the passengers' hearts felt light,
Thinking they would enjoy themselves on the New Year,
With their friends at home they lov'd most dear,
And wish them all a happy New Year.

So the train mov'd slowly along the Bridge of Tay,
Until it was about midway,
Then the central girders with a crash gave way,
And down went the train and passengers into the Tay!
The Storm Fiend did loudly bray,
Because ninety lives had been taken away,
On the last Sabbath day of 1879,
Which will be remember'd for a very long time.

As soon as the catastrophe came to be known
The alarm from mouth to mouth was blown,
And the cry rang out all o'er the town,
Good Heavens! the Tay Bridge is blown down,
And a passenger train from Edinburgh,
Which fill'd all the people's hearts with sorrow,
And made them for to turn pale,
Because none of the passengers were sav'd to tell the tale
How the disaster happen'd on the last Sabbath day of 1879,
Which will be remember'd for a very long time.

It must have been an awful sight,
To witness in the dusky moonlight,
While the Storm Fiend did laugh, and angry did bray,
Along the Railway Bridge of the Silv'ry Tay.
Oh! ill-fated Bridge of the Silv'ry Tay.
I must now conclude my lay
By telling the world fearlessly without the least dismay,
That your central girders would not have given way,

At least many sensible men do say,
Had they been supported on each side with buttresses,
At least many sensible men confesses,
For the stronger we our houses do build,
The less chance we have of being killed.

The Famous Tay Whale

'Twas in the month of December, and in the year 1883,
That a monster whale came to Dundee,
Resolved for a few days to sport and play,
And devour the small fishes in the Silvery Tay.

So the monster whale did sport and play
Among the innocent little fishes in the beautiful Tay,
Until he was seen by some men one day,
And they resolved to catch him without delay.

When it came to be known a whale was seen in the Tay,
Some men began to talk and to say,
We must try and catch this monster of a whale,
So come on, brave boys, and never say fail.

Then the people together in crowds did run,
Resolved to capture the whale and to have some fun!
So small boats were launched on the silvery Tay,
While the monster of the deep did sport and play.

Oh! it was a most fearful and beautiful sight,
To see it lashing the water with its tail all its might,
And making the water ascend like a shower of hail,
With one lash of its ugly and mighty tail.

Then the water did descend on the men in the boats,
Which wet their trousers and also their coats;

But it only made them the more determined to catch
   the whale,
But the whale shook at them his tail.

Then the whale began to puff and to blow,
While the men and the boats after him did go,
Armed well with harpoons for the fray,
Which they fired at him without dismay.

And they laughed and grinned just like wild baboons,
While they fired at him their sharp harpoons:
But when struck with the harpoons he dived below,
Which filled his pursuers' hearts with woe:

Because they guessed they had lost a prize,
Which caused the tears to well up in their eyes;
And in that their anticipations were only right,
Because he sped on to Stonehaven with all his might:

And was first seen by the crew of a Gourdon fishing boat,
Which they thought was a big coble upturned afloat;
But when they drew near they saw it was a whale,
So they resolved to tow it ashore without fail.

So they got a rope from each boat tied round his tail,
And landed their burden at Stonehaven without fail;
And when the people saw it their voices they did raise,
Declaring that the brave fishermen deserved great praise.

And my opinion is that God sent the whale in time of need,
No matter what other people may think or what is
   their creed;
I know fishermen in general are often very poor,
And God in His goodness sent it to drive poverty from
   their door.

So Mr John Wood has bought it for two hundred and
   twenty-six pound,
And has brought it to Dundee all safe and all sound;
Which measures 40 feet in length from the snout to the tail,
So I advise the people far and near to see it without fail.

Then hurrah! for the mighty monster whale,
Which has got 17 feet 4 inches from tip to tip of a tail!
Which can be seen for a sixpence or a shilling,
That is to say, if the people all are willing.

The Funeral
of the
German Emperor

Ye sons of Germany, your noble Emperor William
    now is dead,
Who oft great armies to battle hath led;
He was a man beloved by his subjects all,
Because he never tried them to enthral.

The people of Germany have cause now to mourn
The loss of their hero, who to them will
    ne'er return;
But his soul I hope to Heaven has fled away,
To the realms of endless bliss for ever and aye.

He was much respected throughout Europe by the
    high and the low,
And all over Germany people's hearts are full
    of woe;
For in the battlefield he was a hero bold,
Nevertheless, a lover of peace, to his credit be
    it told.

'Twas in the year of 1888, and on March the
    16th day,
That the peaceful William's remains were
    conveyed away

To the royal mausoleum of Charlottenburg, their
last resting-place,
The God-fearing man that never did his country
disgrace.

The funeral service was conducted in the
cathedral by the court chaplain, Dr. Kogel,
Which touched the hearts of his hearers, as from
his lips it fell,
And in conclusion he recited the Lord's Prayer
In the presence of kings, princes, dukes, and
counts assembled there.

And at the end of the service the infantry outside
fired volley after volley,
While the people inside the cathedral felt
melancholy,
As the sound of the musketry smote upon the ear,
In honour of the illustrious William, whom they
loved most dear.

Then there was a solemn pause as the kings and
princes took their places,
Whilst the hot tears are trickling down their faces,
And the mourners from shedding tears
couldn't refrain;
And in respect of the good man, above the
gateway glared a bituminous flame.

Then the coffin was placed on the funeral car,
By the kings and princes that came from afar;
And the Crown Prince William heads the procession alone,
While behind him are the four heirs-apparent to the throne.

Then followed the three Kings of Saxony, and the King of
the Belgians also,
Together with the Prince of Wales, with their hearts full
of woe,
Besides the Prince of Naples and Prince Rudolph of Austria
were there,
Also the Czarevitch, and other princes in their order I do
declare.

And as the procession passes the palace the blinds are
    drawn completely,
And every house is half hidden with the sable drapery;
And along the line of march expansive arches were erected,
While the spectators standing by seemed very dejected.

And through the Central Avenue, to make the decorations
    complete,
There were pedestals erected, rising fourteen to fifteen feet,
And at the foot and top of each pedestal were hung
    decorations of green bay,
Also beautiful wreaths and evergreen festoons all in grand
    array.
And there were torches fastened on pieces of wood stuck in
    the ground;
And as the people gazed on the weird-like scene, their silence
    was profound;
And the shopkeepers closed their shops, and hotel-keepers
    closed in the doorways,
And with torchlight and gaslight, Berlin for once was all
    ablaze.

The authorities of Berlin in honour of the Emperor
    considered it no sin,
To decorate with crape the beautiful city of Berlin;
Therefore Berlin I declare was a city of crape,
Because few buildings crape decoration did escape.
First in the procession was the Emperor's bodyguard,
And his great love for them nothing could it retard;
Then followed a squadron of the hussars with their band,
Playing "Jesus, Thou my Comfort," most solemn and grand.
And to see the procession passing the sightseers tried
    their best,
Especially when the cavalry hove in sight, riding four abreast;
Men and officers with their swords drawn, a magnificent
    sight to see
In the dim sun's rays, their burnished swords glinting dimly.
Then followed the footguards with slow and solemn tread,
Playing the "Dead March in Saul," most appropriate for
    the dead;

And behind them followed the artillery, with four guns
    abreast,
Also the ministers and court officials dressed in their best.

The whole distance to the grave was covered over with laurel
    and bay,
So that the body should be borne along smoothly all
    the way;
And the thousands of banners in the procession were
    beautiful to view,
Because they were composed of cream-coloured silk and
    light blue.

There were thousands of thousands of men and women
    gathered there,
And standing ankle deep in snow, and seemingly didn't care
So as they got a glimpse of the funeral car,
Especially the poor souls that came from afar.

And when the funeral car appeared there was a general hush,
And the spectators in their anxiety to see began to crush;
And when they saw the funeral car by the Emporer's charger
    led,
Every hat and cap was lifted reverently from off each head.

And as the procession moved on to the royal mausoleum,
The spectators remained bareheaded and seemingly
    quite dumb;
And as the coffin was borne into its last resting-place,
Sorrow seemed depicted in each one's face.

And after the burial service the mourners took a last farewell
Of the noble-hearted William they loved so well;
Then rich and poor dispersed quietly that were assembled
    there,
While two batteries of field-guns fired a salute which did rend
    the air
In honour of the immortal hero they loved so dear,
The founder of the Fatherland Germany, that he did revere.

An Address to the New Tay Bridge

Beautiful new railway bridge of the Silvery Tay,
With your stong brick piers and buttresses in so grand array,
And your thirteen central girders, which seem to my eye
Strong enough all windy storms to defy.
And as I gaze upon thee my heart feels gay,
Because thou are the greatest railway bridge of the
    present day.
And can be seen for miles away
From north, south, east, or west of the Tay
On a beautiful and clear sunshiny day,
And ought to make the hearts of the "Mars" boys feel gay,
Because thine equal nowhere can be seen,
Only near by Dundee and the bonnie Magdalen Green.
Beautiful new railway bridge of the Silvery Tay,
With thy beautiful side-screens along your railway,
Which will be a great protection on a windy day,
So as the railway carriages won't be blown away,
And ought to cheer the hearts of the passengers night
    and day
As they are conveyed along thy beautiful railway,
And towering above the silvery Tay,
Spanning the beautiful river shore to shore
Upwards of two miles and more,
Which is most wonderful to be seen
Near by Dundee and the Bonnie Magdalen Green.
Thy structure to my eye seems strong and grand,
And the workmanship most skilfully planned;
And I hope the designers, Messrs Barlow & Arrol, will
    prosper for many a day
For erecting thee across the beautiful Tay.
And I think nobody need have the least dismay
To cross o'er thee by night or by day,
Because thy strength is visible to be seen
Near by Dundee and the bonnie Magdalen Green.

Beautiful new railway bridge of the Silvery Tay,
I wish you success for many a year and a day,
And I hope thousands of people will come from far away,
Both high and low without delay,
From the north, south, east, and the west,
Because as a railway bridge thou are the best;
Thou standest unequalled to be seen
Near by Dundee and the bonnie Magdalen Green.

And for beauty thou art most lovely to be seen
As the train crosses o'er thee with her cloud of steam;
And you look well, painted the colour of marone,
And to find thy equal there is none,
Which, without fear of contradiction, I venture to say,
Because you are the longest railway bridge of the present day
That now crosses o'er a tidal river stream,
And the most handsome to be seen
Near by Dundee and the bonnie Magdalen Green.

The New Yorkers boast about their Brooklyn Bridge,
But in comparison to thee it seems like a midge,
Because thou spannest the silvery Tay
A mile and more longer I venture to say;
Besides the railway carriages are pulled across by a rope,
Therefore Brooklyn Bridge cannot with thee cope;
And as you have been opened on the 20th day of June,
I hope Her Majesty Queen Victoria will visit thee very soon,
Because thou are worthy of a visit from Duke, Lord,
    or Queen,
And strong and securely built, which is most worthy to
    be seen
Near by Dundee and the bonnie Magdalen Green.

The Sprig of Moss

There lived in Munich a poor, weakly youth,
But for the exact date, I cannot vouch for the truth,
And of seven of a family he was the elder,
Who was named, by his parents, Alois Senefelder.

But, poor fellow, at home his father was lying dead,
And his little brothers and sisters were depending upon him
  for bread,
And one evening he was dismissed from his employment,
Which put an end to all his peace and enjoyment.

The poor lad was almost mad, and the next day
His parent's remains to the cemetery were taken away;
And when his father was buried, distracted like he grew,
And he strolled through the streets crying, What shall I do!

And all night he wandered on sad and alone,
Until he began to think of returning home,
But, to his surprise, on raising his head to look around,
He was in a part of the country which to him was unknown
  ground.

And when night came on the poor lad stood aghast,
For all was hushed save the murmuring of a river which
  flowed past;
And the loneliness around seemed to fill his heart with awe,
And, with fatigue, he sat down on the first stone he saw.

And there resting his elbows and head on his knees,
He sat gazing at the running water, which did him please;
And by the light of the stars which shone on the water blue,
He cried, I will drown myself, and bid this harsh world adieu.

Besides, I'm good for nothing, to himself he said,
And will only become a burden to my mother, I'm afraid;
And there, at the bottom of that water, said he,
From all my misfortunes death will set me free.

But, happily for Alois, more pious thoughts rushed into
  his mind,
And courage enough to drown himself he couldn't find,
So he resolved to go home again whatever did betide,
And he asked forgiveness of his Creator by the river side.

And as he knelt, a few incoherent words escaped him,
And the thought of drowning himself he considered a
  great sin,

And the more he thought of it, he felt his flesh creep,
But in a few minutes he fell fast asleep.

And he slept soundly, for the stillness wasn't broke,
And the day was beginning to dawn before he awoke;
Then suddenly he started up as if in a fright,
And he saw very near him a little stone smooth and white,

Upon which was traced the delicate design of a Sprig
    of Moss
But to understand such a design he was at a loss,
Then he recollected the Sprig of Moss lying on the stone,
And with his tears he'd moistened it, but it was gone.

But its imprint was delicately imprinted on the stone;
Then, taking the stone under his arm, he resolved to
    go home,
Saying, God has reserved me for some other thing,
And with joy he couldn't tell how he began to sing.

And on drawing near the city he met his little brother,
Who told him his uncle had visited his mother,
And on beholding their misery had left them money to
    buy food,
Then Alois cried, Thank God, the news is good!

Then 'twas on the first day after Alois came home,
He began the printing of the Sprig of Moss on the stone;
And by taking the impressions of watch-cases he discovered
    one day,
What is now called the art of Lithography.

So Alois plodded on making known his great discovery,
Until he obtained the notice of the Royal Academy,
Besides, he obtained a gold Medal, and what was more dear
to his heart,
He lived to see the wide extension of his art.

And when life's prospects may at times appear dreary to ye,
Remember Alois Senefelder, the discoverer of Lithography

How God saved him from drowning himself in adversity,
And I hope ye all will learn what the Sprig of Moss
    teaches ye.

And God that made a way through the Red Sea,
If ye only put your trust in Him, He will protect ye,
And light up your path, and strew it with flowers,
And be your own Comforter in all your lonely hours.

A Tribute to Henry M. Stanley

Welcome, thrice welcome, to the City of Dundee
The great African explorer, Henry M. Stanley,
Who went out to Africa its wild regions to explore,
And travelled o'er wild and lonely deserts, fatigued
    and footsore.

And what he and his little band suffered will never be forgot,
Especially one in particular, Major Edmund Barttelot,
Alas! the brave heroic officer by a savage was shot,
The commandant of the rear column—O hard has been
    his lot!

O think of the noble Stanley and his gallant little band,
While travelling through gloomy forests and devastated land,
And suffering from all kinds of hardships under a burning
    sun!
But the brave hero has been successful, and the victory's
    won!

While in Africa he saw many wonderful sights,
And was engaged, no doubt, in many savage fights,
But the wise Creator was with him all along,
And now he's home again to us, I hope quite strong.

And during his travels in Africa he made strange discoveries,
He discovered a dwarfish race of people called pigmies,
Who are said to be the original natives of Africa,
And when Stanley discovered them he was struck with awe.

One event in particular is most worthy to relate,
How God preserved him from a very cruel fate:
He and his officers were attacked, while sailing their boat,
By the savages of Bumbireh, all eager to cut his throat.

They seized him by the hair,and tugged it without fear,
While one of his men received a poke in the ribs with
   a spear;
But Stanley, having presence of mind, instantly contrives
To cry to his men, Shove off the boat, and save your lives!

Then savages swarmed into three canoes very close by,
And every bow was drawn, while they savagely did cry;
But the heroic Stanley quickly shot two of them dead,
Then the savages were baffled, and immediately fled.

This incident is startling, but nevertheless true,
And in the midst of all dangers the Lord brought him through
Then, welcome him, thrice welcome him, right cheerfully,
Shouting, Long live the great African explorer, Henry
   M. Stanley!

Therefore throw open the gates of the City of Dundee,
And receive him with loud cheers, three times three,
And sound your trumpets and beat your drums,
And play up, See the Conquering Hero Comes!
